# Archives of the Masters of Arms of Paris

# Archives of the Masters of Arms of Paris

*Les Archives des Maîtres d'Armes de Paris*

Henri Daressy

translated by Chris Slee

**Archives of the Masters of Arms of Paris**
Copyright ©2018 Chris Slee (translator)

ISBN: 978-0-9943590-9-4 (eBook)
ISBN: 978-0-9943590-8-7 (Print)

All Rights Reserved. No part of this publication may be reproduced, stored in a retrieval system, or transmitted, in any form or in any means – by electronic, mechanical, photocopying, recording or otherwise – without prior written permission from the copyright owner(s).

*Les Archives des Maîtres d'Armes de Paris*, Henri Daressy. The original text is from a facsimile of the 1888 edition. It is asserted this book is in the public domain.

Created at LongEdge Press, first edition.

# Contents

Introduction ix
    The Corporation . . . . . . . . . . . . . . . . . . . . . . . . . ix
    Henry Daressy . . . . . . . . . . . . . . . . . . . . . . . . . . xi
    The Text . . . . . . . . . . . . . . . . . . . . . . . . . . . . xi
    The Translation . . . . . . . . . . . . . . . . . . . . . . . . xiii
    References . . . . . . . . . . . . . . . . . . . . . . . . . . . xiv

Preface 3

Historical Overview 5

Notes on the Historical Overview 13

Ordinances and Statutes of the Master Players and Sword Fencers of the City of Paris for the Regulation of the Said Fencing 23

Ordinances of the Masters of Deeds of Arms of the City of Paris 27

Statutes and Rules made by the Masters of Deeds of Arms of the Town and Suburbs of Paris for the Support of their Privileges granted by Kings 33

Letters Patent 43
    (December 1567) . . . . . . . . . . . . . . . . . . . . . . . . 43
    (December 1585) . . . . . . . . . . . . . . . . . . . . . . . . 44
    (March 1635) . . . . . . . . . . . . . . . . . . . . . . . . . . 47
    (September 1643) . . . . . . . . . . . . . . . . . . . . . . . . 50
    (May 1656) . . . . . . . . . . . . . . . . . . . . . . . . . . . 55
    (December 1758) . . . . . . . . . . . . . . . . . . . . . . . . 58

**Judgement Against Vincent Banvarelle**    61

**Judgements Against the Master of Arms Called *Ferrailleurs***    63
    (18 December 1685) . . . . . . . . . . . . . . . . . . . . . . . 63
    (18 December 1685) . . . . . . . . . . . . . . . . . . . . . . . 64
    (23 June 1724) . . . . . . . . . . . . . . . . . . . . . . . . . . . 64
    (14 June 1765) . . . . . . . . . . . . . . . . . . . . . . . . . . . 65
    Court Injunctions Concerning Colleges and Boarding Houses   65

**Masters of Arms of Paris (1556–1850)**    67
    List of the Masters of Arms . . . . . . . . . . . . . . . . . . 71
    List of Masters of the Royal School of Arms of the City of
        Paris who have made a Patriotic Offering of their Swords   78
        Nineteenth Century . . . . . . . . . . . . . . . . . . . . . 81
    Principle Masters of Arms of Some Towns of France . . . . 84
        Nineteenth Century . . . . . . . . . . . . . . . . . . . . . 85

**Fencing and Fencers (1556–1850)**    87
    Sale by Mathieu Gossu to Jean Gossu . . . . . . . . . . . . . 87
    Letter of Permission for Mathieu De Lor . . . . . . . . . . . 87
    Warrant Accorded to Laurent Fontaine . . . . . . . . . . . 88
    Receptions of Masters and Elections of *Jurés* . . . . . . . . 88
    Cavalcabo . . . . . . . . . . . . . . . . . . . . . . . . . . . . . . 90
    Jacques Ferron . . . . . . . . . . . . . . . . . . . . . . . . . . . 91
    Essay on the Marvels of Nature . . . . . . . . . . . . . . . . 92
        The Use of Arms . . . . . . . . . . . . . . . . . . . . . . . . 92
    A Fencing Competition at Toulouse . . . . . . . . . . . . . 97
    The Master of Arms by Bonnart . . . . . . . . . . . . . . . 97
    Pierre Daniel . . . . . . . . . . . . . . . . . . . . . . . . . . . . 98
    Bertrand Teillagorry . . . . . . . . . . . . . . . . . . . . . . . 98
        Declaration of Cens . . . . . . . . . . . . . . . . . . . . . . 98
    Dorcy . . . . . . . . . . . . . . . . . . . . . . . . . . . . . . . . . 98
    Lefebvre, His Provost Warrant Annulled . . . . . . . . . . 99
    Guillaume Danet . . . . . . . . . . . . . . . . . . . . . . . . . 99
    La Boëssière, senior . . . . . . . . . . . . . . . . . . . . . . . 100
        The Noble Death Of Prince Léopold of Brunswick . . 101
        Preface . . . . . . . . . . . . . . . . . . . . . . . . . . . . . . 101
        The Cry of Vengeance on the Breaking of the Peace
            and the Infamy of the English Ministers . . . . 104
    The Knight Saint-George . . . . . . . . . . . . . . . . . . . 105
        Account of Musicians Used in Spectacles for the Service of Monseigneur . . . . . . . . . . . . . . . . 107

Augustin Rousseau . . . . . . . . . . . . . . . . . . . . . . . . 108
    Letter addressed to Citizen Antoine, the Pavillion be-
        fore Orléans, 21 rue de Union, at Versailles. . . 110
Three Masters of Arms become Marshals of France . . . . . 111
Bouting in the Gardens of the Palais-Royale . . . . . . . . . 112
Charlemagne . . . . . . . . . . . . . . . . . . . . . . . . . . . 112
Jean Daressy . . . . . . . . . . . . . . . . . . . . . . . . . . . 112
La Boëssière, junior . . . . . . . . . . . . . . . . . . . . . . 114
Lafaugère . . . . . . . . . . . . . . . . . . . . . . . . . . . . . 115
Jean-Louis . . . . . . . . . . . . . . . . . . . . . . . . . . . . 119
Bertrand. . . . . . . . . . . . . . . . . . . . . . . . . . . . . . 120
Assault of Arms in 1814 . . . . . . . . . . . . . . . . . . . . 121
Pierre Daressy . . . . . . . . . . . . . . . . . . . . . . . . . . 123
Academy of Arms (1886) . . . . . . . . . . . . . . . . . . . . 126

**Duels and Letters of Remission**     **127**
    Duel between François de Vivonne, Lord of Chateigneraie
        and Guy Chabot, Baron of Jarnac . . . . . . . . . . . . 127
        The Coup de Jarnac . . . . . . . . . . . . . . . . . . . 129
    The Duel of a Seventeen-Year-Old Page (1540) . . . . . . . 131
    The Duel of Des Bordes against d'Ivoy-Genlis (1560) . . . . 131
    Letter of Challenge from Lord Castel-Bayart . . . . . . . . 131
    Letter Addressed to the Tribunal of the Marshals of France . 132
    Admonition Obtained by the Baron of Gourgue . . . . . . 132
    Letter of Pardon Accorded to Etienne de Clugny of Praslay,
        Councillor in the Court of the Parliament of Dijon . . 133

**139**

# Introduction

## The Corporation

The Corporation of the Masters in Deeds of Arms of Paris was founded in 1567 by Charles IX in response to being petitioned by the fencing teachers in the city. It regulated fencing schools until the corporation was disbanded by the Revolutionary Council in 1791. In 1827, some time after the restoration of the Bourbons, the guild was revived as an anaemic shadow of its former glory as the King's Academy of Fencing and it continues today as the *Académie d'Armes de France* – even using the same heraldry presented to the Corporation by Louis XIV in 1656.

At its creation, the corporation was a collection of individuals practising the same craft and was structured in a similar manner to other artisanal guilds of the time. The key objective of the organisation was to regulate who was permitted to teach fencing and related activities in the city and surrounds of Paris. In other words, the masters were protecting their incomes.

The initial charter of 1567 made provision for two *Gardes* of the Corporation who were appointed by the vote of the membership and held office for two years. The two-year terms were staggered such that each year one *Garde* was elected. They were responsible for ensuring that the ordinances and regulations pertaining to the conduct of the corporation, the masters and their students were adhered to and reporting any breaches to the crown. The charter was amended in 1633 to introduce a perpetual *Syndic* or Trustee whose job it was to oversee the enforcement of the Statutes. This structure remained largely untouched until the Revolution.

Several refinements to the Corporation's charter were made during the period of its existence. Henry III, by his Letters Patent of 1585, increased the length of time a fencer must serve as provost from two years to four before he may attempt his prize play to become a master. In the charter of 1633, a religious test was imposed on all candidates for the Mastery, refusing entry to any except Catholics, and the length of service required of a provost was increased to its final duration of six years. It may be that the religious test was previously assumed and no one saw the need to state it as a criterion. In 1644, in rewriting the charter from scratch, a minimum age was introduced of 25 years for new masters and 22 years for sons of masters. A provision was made for masters to absent themselves on business for up to one year and three months and have their fencing hall or *salle d'armes* (or simply salle) taught by another. After this time, if they have not returned to teach again in person, the Trustees of the Corporation may order the salle closed.

However, the primary use of the Corporation's charters was to prosecute anyone not a member from teaching fencing in Paris and surrounds. This is reflected in several court decisions against individual *ferailleurs* reproduced in the book and by several provisions in the revised charters. These decisions come in three distinct categories. The first, the easiest, is the injunctions taken out against *ferailleurs* who set themselves up as fencing teachers without being recognised by the Corporation. The second type, related to the first, concerns those fencing teachers, having received "Letters of Mastery" from various nobles, including at times the King himself, who consider themselves Masters of Arms without having fulfilled the entry requirements outlined in the Corporation's charter. More complex is the final type which deals with the provision in the original charter of 1567 which permitted the widows of fencing masters to continue to run their late husband's salle if they could find a "suitably qualified" fencer to teach it. The welfare of the widows and families of members was one of the driving factors behind the formation of the medieval guilds. However, in this case, it apparently led to several salles being taught by fencers who were not members of the Corporation. One of the difficulties they faced in regulating this related to the various men who taught fencing to sections of the royal household, such as Jean Pillard, fencing master to the pages of the King's Stables. There are several allusions to injunctions restricting their teaching activities to within the scope of their office (in Pillard's case, the Stables) and disallowing any attempt to open a salle to the Parisian public.

The Corporation ended in the Revolution. In 1789, representatives of the Corporation presented themselves before the National Assembly to swear allegiance to the state and offer their skills to train the next generation and to defend liberty from absolutism. This only delayed the inevitable. On 17 March 1791, all the former masteries, corporations and guilds were suppressed and disbanded. The one holdout, the Royal School of Arms started by Guillaume Danet in his own house in 1788, endured until it too was closed in 1792.

The Revolution was a dangerous time for the fencing masters so closely associated with the *Ancien Régime*. Augustin Rousseau was executed by the Revolutionary Council in July 1794. Daressy reproduces Rousseau's final letter to his family written the night before his trial and subsequent execution.

## Henry Daressy

Daressy (b. 1835) was born into a fencing dynasty. Himself a noted fencer with an evident strong interest in the history and development of fencing, it is, however, to his father and grandfather we look to better understand the man.

Henry's father, Pierre (1806-1871), won the position of fencing master to the Royal Guards Regiment at the age of twenty-three. In this role, he fought a public bout with François-Joseph Bertrand, one of the most celebrated fencing masters in France during the nineteenth century, without the latter able to better him. He opened his own salle after leaving military service which he ran until 1860, five years after developing blindness caused by cataracts. Even blind, he taught based on *sentiment-de-fer* alone.

Jean-Anselme Daressy (1770-1821), Henry's grandfather, learned to fence in Agen (between Toulouse and Bordeaux) under Blondin before joining the 12th Hussars Regiment in 1793. On demobilising in 1800, he opened a fencing school in his home town. Among his many famous students was Louis-Justin Lafaugère, author of a *Traité de l'art de faire des armes* [Treatise on the Art of Using Arms] in 1820.

Henry's son, Georges-Émile-Jules Daressy (1864-1938), broke with family tradition and as an Egyptologist won fame for translating the Akhmim tablets, a mathematical textbook from the Middle Kingdom period dating to approximately 1950 BC.

## The Text

This is not an organised study but a collection of random documents sorted into a couple of discrete piles. The documents collected in the book do not represent the entirety of the Archives. Some documents have been lost forever. Also, these documents do not represent the entirety of the corpus of historical material relating to fencing in Paris and France in the time before the Revolution. For example, there are several ordinances, injunctions and letters of remission quoted and copied verbatim in La Beraudiere's treatise on duelling and duel management, *Le combat de seul à seul en camp clos* [One on One Combat in the Lists] (1608), and in Jean Savaron's history of and polemic against judicial combat, *Traicté contre les duels* [Tract Against Duelling] (1610).

Daressy does not clearly explain how his collection of documents came to be nor his efforts in tracking down the documents. It appears that he was possessed of antiquarian tendencies and picked each up as it appeared or came to his notice. A review of the book in *Gil Blas*,[1] a Parisian literary daily newspaper, confirms the haphazard nature of the collection while highlighting Daressy's diligence.

> P.S.- Signalling to sportsmen two or three interesting publications, amongst others *The Archives of the Masters of Arms of Paris* by M. Henry Daressy. It's a very well-made work that we recommend to all persons interested in fencing curiosities. M. Daressy is a swordsman of the first order who, during thirty years, never missed[2] an opportunity to collect anything that could have related[3] to the Company of the Master of Arms of Paris and it is thanks to this work and patience that he has come to reconstitute almost entirely the history of this Company.

The documents collected here give a very good understanding of the shape and processes of the Corporation of the Master of Arms of Paris during its 225-year history. We see how the corporation's charter changed over time and gain an insight into some of the – presumably – more significant legal battles it faced as masters and members sued to protect their privileges and the status of the corporation. It is not surprising that the lists of masters are filled with famous names and the names of men who have shaped fencing history and continue to strongly influence modern HEMA.

---

[1] Vol. 10, No. 3108, 22 May 1888, p.3
[2] *n'a jamais laissé perdue*
[3] *tout ce qui pouvait avait trait*

## The Translation

I have maintained the material in the order it appears in Daressy's book with one exception. I have moved his Notes on the Historical Overview chapter from its original location at the end of the ill-defined *premiere partie* to immediately follow the overview. Without a clearly indicated gap between the parts of the book, the original sequence of chapters appears even more disjointed.

The language of the legal documents in the first part of the book is positively torturous as, I imagine, should be expected. The sheer number of nested dependent clauses, sometimes up to five layers deep, makes untangling the meaning of a passage very difficult. To what noun – either preceding or to come – does this pronoun refer? This is especially evident in the seventeenth century documents. I have at times broken these overly long strings of words into shorter sentences to assist the reader.

I do not have full confidence in my translation of some of these documents. A specialist in medieval and early modern French law may have better luck translating them.

Text enclosed in parentheses ( ) appeared so in the original book. Text enclosed in square brackets [ ] are my interpolations. Personal name suffixes such as *père, fils, aîné,* and *jeune* have been translated as senior, junior, the elder, and the younger. The then current method for listing names – Last Name (First Name) – has been retained in most instances. Inconsistencies in the capitalisation of names and titles in the original text has also been retained.

These job titles and administrative terms have provided some difficulties.

*Syndic* may be translated as trustee or similar. The concept is of a person with an interest in the long-term trajectory of the organisation who can keep the organisation faithful to its vision. A modern equivalent may be the chairman of a company's Board of Directors, responsible for the organisation's outlook five or more years into the future and not concerned with its day to day affairs.

*Juré* is a complex term involving the idea of a sworn member of a guild or other organisation whose chief task is to ensure that the rules and regulations of the body are maintained. Generally, a *juré* is a member required to swear an oath in order to achieve the position. It is not conferred simply by length of service or by generating respect within the community or some other criteria.

*Garde de l'Ordre* (or simply *Garde*) is another role dedicated to ensuring that the rules and regulations of the organisation are kept by its members. Exactly how this role differs from that of the *juré* is unclear. Perhaps they are job titles separated more by historical period rather than by function.

*Brevet* is complex term with no direct translation into English. I have often translated it as license, permission or warrant, as required to assist understanding the term in context, showing the bearer is permitted to perform a function or entitled to a privilege. It also covers the idea of a certificate of accomplishment awarded after the completion of an activity.

*Procurer, Procurer Général, Procurator, Procurator Général* all refer to the office which we would call the Attorney-General, the chief law officer of the state and the legal advisor to the king. The inconsistencies of spelling and title even within the same document force me for clarity to settle on transcribing all instances to Procurer General.

My translation of René François' entry on "The Use of Arms" in the *Essay des Merveilles de Nature* [Essay on the Marvels of Nature] (1622) previously appeared on the HROARR website.[4]

# References

Cayla, J. M. (1853). *Histoire des arts et métiers et des corporations ouvrières de la ville de Paris depuis les temps les plus reculés jusqu'à nos jours* [History of the Arts and Trades and Worker Corporations of the Town of Paris from the Earliest Times to Our Day]. Lagny.

Daressy, H. (1867). *Statuts et règlements faits par les maîtres en faits d'armes de la ville et fauxbourgs de Paris, 1644* [Statutes and Regulation made by the Masters of Arms of the Town and Suburbs of Paris, 1644]. Vasseur Libraire.

Dupuis, O. (2016). "The French fighting traditions from the 14th century to 1630 in fight books". In Jaquet, D., Verelst, K., and Dawson, T., editors, *Late Medieval and Early Modern Fight Books: Transmission and Tradition of Martial Arts in Europe (14th-17th Centuries)*, History of Warfare. Brill.

Epstein, S. and Prak, M. (2008). *Guilds, Innovation and the European Economy, 1400–1800*. Cambridge University Press.

François, R. (pseudonym for Binnet, E.). (1622). *Essay des Merveilles de Nature* [Essay on the Marvels of Nature]. R. de Beauvais & I. Osmont.

---

[4] https://hroarr.com/article/the-use-of-weapons-rene-francois-1621/

Goudourville, H. (1899). *Escrimeurs contemporains* [Contemporary Fencers]. Chamuel.

Kessler, A. (2007). *A Revolution in Commerce: The Parisian Merchant Court and the Rise of Commercial Society in Eighteenth-century France.* Yale University Press.

La Beraudiere, M. de. (1608). *Le combat de seul à seul en camp clos* [One on One Combat in the Lists]. Abel l'Angelier.

Labadie, E. (1902). *Les Maîtres d'armes bordelais du XVIIIe siècle* [The Masters of Arms of Bordeaux in the 18th Century]. M. Mounastre-Picamilh.

Lafaugère, L. J. (1820). *Traité de l'Art de Faire des Armes* [Treatise on the Art of Using Arms]. Chez l'auteur.

Lespinasse, R. (1897). *Les métiers et corporations de la ville de Paris* [Trades and Companies of the Town of Paris], volume 3 of *Histoire générale de Paris* [General History of Paris]. Imprimerie nationale.

Letainturier-Fradin, G. (1905). *Les joueurs d'épée à travers les siècles* [Swordsmen Across the Centuries]. E. Flammarion.

Savaron, J. (1610). *Traicté contre les duels* [Tract Against Duels]. Périer. Paris.

Tavernier, A. (1886). *Amateurs et salles d'armes de Paris* [Amateurs and Fencing Halls of Paris]. C. Marpon et E.Flammarion

Vigeant, A. (1882). *La bibliographie de l'escrime ancienne et moderne* [Bibliography of Ancient and Modern Fencing]. Imprimé par Motteroz.

# Archives of the Masters of Arms of Paris

Henry Daressy

# Preface

The son and grandson of masters of arms, we were interested early in all that which could give us useful or interesting information on the art that, guided by the vigilant care of our father, we have cultivated for nearly twenty years in an amateur capacity.

We have collected treatises and engravings relating to fencing but, above all, it is documents of the former Community of the Masters of Arms of Paris that we have researched with passion.[5]

In 1791, all the corporations, guilds and masteries[6] having been abolished, the Company of the Masters of Arms suffered the same fate and its archives, henceforth without purpose, were dispersed and in part lost. From time to time, we have had the good fortune to reunite some jetsam that escaped the shipwreck and for thirty years we have never lost an opportunity to increase our collection.

With the help both of our documents and of the notes obtained from the National Archives and from public and private libraries, we were able to reconstruct nearly entirely the history of the Company, which is the constant object of our studies.

We believe [it] to be agreeable to persons interested in the curiosities of fencing published in the present book, the results of our researches, [that] we would be happy to see it take its place, a modest title, beside the *Bibliographie de l'escrime ancienne et moderne* [Bibliography of Ancient and Modern Fencing] made by one of our great modern masters, at once a charming storyteller and researcher, passionate about old treatises of arms: we have named Vigeant.[7]

---

[5] Original footnote: Under the title Statutes and Rules made by the Masters of deeds of arms of the city and suburbs of Paris we published in 1867 some notes concerning this Company

[6] *maîtrises privilégiées* – higher level guilds composed solely of those having completed their master-work

[7] Arsène Vigeant (1844-1916), fencer and historian of fencing, one of the brightest celebrities of the Parisian fencing scene in the late 19th century and fencing master to Napoleon III.

The reader will follow in the first part of our work the history of the various transformations undergone by the Statutes of the Master Players and Sword Fencers,[8] becoming later the Masters in Deeds of Arms of the King's Academies.

Following the Statutes are added the Letters Patent accorded to the Community by the kings of France, some judgements and injunctions, and finally the names of the principle Masters of Arms having taught in France from 1556 to 1850.

The second part contains some information on fencing and fencers from different periods, some notes concerning duels and Letters of Remission.

In the chapter dedicated to the celebrated duel of La Chateignerie and Jarnac, we have tried to show, contrary to the erroneous opinion commonly held, that the conduct of the latter gentleman had been perfectly honourable: French honour created this duty for us.

Giving in to filial sentiment, we give the biography of our grandfather, Jean Daressy, Lafaugère's master, and of Pierre Daressy, our father.

Their memory sustained us in the accomplishment of the task that we undertook. We dedicate this book to their memory.

---

[8] *les Statuts des Maistres Joueurs et Escrimeurs d'Espée*

# Historical Overview

We have little information on the Master of Arms of Paris during the Middle Ages and even until the middle of the 16th century. The oldest document where they may be mentioned, to our knowledge, dates from the reign of Philippe le Bel.[9]

This is the roll of the tax levied in 1291[10] on the inhabitants of Paris. We find in this piece the names, dwellings, as well as the tax paid by each of the seven *escrémisséeurs*.[11]

The 16th century being the point of departure of our publication, we will start the series of documents with the Ordinance of 1554.

In this period, the scholars of the University readily abandoned the study of Greek and Latin to fence in the *salles d'armes*. An ordinance of Parliament, dated 20 August 1554, concerning the police of the University scholars,[12] carries in its Article VI that "several of the said scholars instead of attending to their studies often go to the houses of the master fencers and sword players living in the said suburbs[13] or to secluded places[14] for fear of the being seen by their masters and guardians." In order to remediate this state of things, the Court enjoined "all the said fencers and sword players to withdraw themselves into the said town, and the public streets of which, from this moment on holding themselves and dwelling in the said suburbs, on pain on imprisonment or other arbitrary fine."

We do not know if this Article VI had the effect of further retaining the scholars on college benches.

Until 1567, the Masters of Arms of Paris held themselves isolated

---

[9] Philip IV (April–June 1268 – 29 November 1314), called the Fair (French: *Philippe le Bel*) or the Iron King (French: *le Roi de fer*), was King of France from 1285 until his death
[10] Original footnote: 1. The numbers refer to the Notes on the Historical Overview
[11] Original footnote: 2
[12] Original footnote: 3
[13] Original footnote: 4
[14] *lieux destournez*

from each other. But understanding the advantage that they could have in forming a privileged company, they set down the statutes that they submitted for Royal sanction. Charles IX,[15] by his Letters Patent of the month of December 1567, authorised the *Maistres Joueurs et Escrimeurs d'épée* of the city of Paris to assemble[16] and confirm their statutes.

In 1573, Henry de Sainct-Didier,[17] a gentleman of Pertuis in Provence, published the first work in French treating on the science of arms. He dedicated it to King Charles IX.

At the request of this prince, the author bouted with a brother of the King and also with the Duke de Guise.[18]

Clarified by experience, the Community of Master Fencers recognised the faults in certain articles of the rules. They corrected their statues and presented them for the king's approval.

Henri III, by his Letters Patent of the month of December 1585, confirmed all the privileges accorded by Charles IX, and in order to give more authority to the Community, he had the reformed statutes registered by Parliament (27 January 1586).

The amendments had the aim of: 1) of extending from two to four years the period of apprenticeship necessary in order for provosts before presenting themselves for the masters exam;[19] 2) forbidding all persons from teaching the exercise of arms unless they had received their mastery by masterpiece or examination; 3) removing from the widows of masters the right to serve in place of the deceased in order to maintain a fencing hall.

That which motivated this last reform is that instead of conforming themselves to the rules which prescribed that widows take the provosts imposed by the Guards of the Mastery,[20] it happened several times that they took the first comers, even without certificates of competency.

On the occasion of a joyous event, a birth, a marriage of prince or princess, also often as a gracious gift, the kings and queens of France created Letters of Mastery in each of the communities of arts and professions. Those that were granted in the Community of the Masters of Arms often became a cause for litigation between the Community, jealous of respecting their privileges, and the possessors of these new

---

[15] Original footnote: 5

[16] *se réunir en communauté*

[17] Original footnote: 6

[18] Original footnote: 7

[19] *la maîtrise* – the process of graduating from provost to master, translated here as the Mastery or master's exam

[20] *les Gardes de la maîtrise*

Letters, these latter absolutely refusing to make the examination demanded by the statutes, claiming to have the right of exercising their profession freely and without any control.

Such was the case of an Italian master named Vincent Vannarelli,[21] provided by Queen Marie de Médici with one of these Letters of Mastery. He did not want to submit to the regulated masterpiece and began litigation with the Community on 10 July 1619. An injunction of Parliament, given on 12 August 1621, forbade him exercising before having made a "light examination with six masters and with four types of weapons."[22]

In 1633, the Community set down new Ordinances in order to re-establish order in the reception of masters, often accepted outside the established rules "from too great a charity and accommodation by us all," says these Ordinances.

The period of apprenticeship was increased to six years in place of four, and it was only after the first two years had passed that the provost could wear the ordinary sword (?)[23] with the permission, nonetheless, of the trustee and the master who taught them arms.

The masters took the formal commitment of no longer obliging any provost who was not a native of the kingdom of France. (To oblige, that is to say, to prepare for the Mastery.)

Saint Michael being the patron of fencers, all the members of the Community must, according to the new Ordinances, visit the great Augustinian monastery on the saint's feast day, in order to hear mass celebrated in his honour, "under pain of an *écu*[24] if he has not legitimate excuse." This annual mass was previously said in the church of Sainte-Geneviève-des-Ardents (located on rue Neuve-Notre-Dame).

In the Letters Patent given at Chantilly in March 1635, paying tribute to the progress in teaching fencing made by members of the Community, Louis XIII states "that by means of the great care, work and diligence of the masters exercising in our good city of Paris, the exercise and test of arms have come to such a degree of perfection that whereas in the past our subjects used to go to foreign countries in order to learn the said exercise and handling of arms, now, foreigners are obliged to come to France for this effect."[25]

By these Letters Patent, Louis XIII exempted the Community from any Letters of Mastery which could be created in the future and

---

[21] Original footnote: 8
[22] Original footnote: 9
[23] *l'épée ordinaire*
[24] a small gold coin
[25] Original footnote: 10

quashed[26] and annulled all those which had been accorded up until this period.

Despite his edict, King Louis XIII himself gave to Jean Pillard, fencing master to his grooms, Letters and a warrant of permission in 1637 and in 1642.

Jean Pillard wanted to open a fencing hall in the city of Paris but the Community opposed it. A trial followed which ended with the Injunction of the Grand Council, given 14 July 1643, which enjoined Jean Pillard to close his hall and to not teach his art outside the king's stables.

On 30 September 1643, Louis XIV confirmed the Statutes, Rules and Ordinances of the Company as well as the Sentences and Injunctions made in favour of the Community.

In the month of May 1644, the Masters of Arms made new statutes. Article 14 stated that a master could not absent himself from this fencing hall for private business for more than a year and three months, which, this time passed, the *Jurés* and the *Gardes* could close the hall, "and that if it were for exercising some office which contravenes the nobility and dignity of the said art, he will not only be obliged to close his said hall as early as it may be permitted by the contravening Office but also to renounce this profession."

Louis XIV gave other Letters Patent to the Community in the month of May 1656. He wanted that in the future the number of masters of deeds of arms in the city, suburbs and outskirts of Paris, which were twenty-five, be reduced to twenty.

The king granted hereditary nobility to the six oldest masters having twenty years practice since their reception to the mastery. After the death of one of them, the oldest master succeeded him, and, at the start of his twentieth year of practice, he should be ennobled in his turn, and so on.

The king forbade any person not having been a provost under one of the Masters of the Company of exercising the profession of master of arms within the extent of his kingdom.

He granted to the Company the following coat of arms: "a field of azure with two swords saltire, the points high, the pommels, handles and cross guards of gold, accompanied by four fleurs-de-lys with decorations[27] above the crest and trophies of arms all around."

The first masters named to take advantage of the privileges of the new edict were Jehan or Jean Le Coq and Jean Renard, lord of Préville, ennobling both 28 February 1657. Jean Renard is the master who

---

[26] *cassa*

[27] *timbre*

signed Regnard on the statutes of 1644. He was also *Juré* for the second time.

By the marks of favour granted to the Company of the Masters of Arms of Paris, the king demonstrated the importance which he attached to the teaching of fencing.

Louis XIV himself started, from the age of ten years, to practice fencing under the direction of Vincent de Saint-Ange.[28] Pascal Rousseau was the second master to the king.

In the 17th century, people who taught fencing without being part of the Community were called "*ferrailleurs*."[29]

On 18 December 1685, a judgement given at the request of the King's Procurer forbade one named Bary, *ferrailleur*, from insinuating himself into the exercise of the masters of deeds of arms and ordered the closure of his fencing hall. Bary had been surprised "demonstrating the exercise of deeds of arms, foil in hand, sandals and slippers on the feet."

Two similar injunctions were given the same day against two other *ferrailleurs* named l'Hoste and Caudat.

Despite the severity of these judgements, the Company of the Masters of Arms was obliged several times to resort[30] to magistrates in order to check the growth of the *ferrailleurs*. Notably, in December 1722, ten commissioners of police were charged with reporting against Rouet, Houaley, Nègre, Lépine, Lemaire, Hénault, Duplessis, Peirière, Sinègre, Keilly father and son, Le Petit Basque, La Jeunesse, Ramé and Esborel, all masters of arms without status.[31]

On 23 June 1724, a police judgement given by Gabriel-Hyérome de Bullion, Provost of Paris, forbade *ferrailleurs* to train under pain of a 300 livre fine, confiscation of foils, plastrons, etc, and even of imprisonment.

It was forbidden for any landlord or principal tenant to rent to any person calling himself a master of arms without being presented with the Letter of Mastery and the act of reception made by oath before the king's procurer under penalty of a 200 livre fine and the immediate closing of the fencing hall which must remain shut[32] for six months.

This judgement also forbade also wine merchants, beer and spirits sellers to allow in their courtyards and gardens any assembly on the part of the *ferrailleurs* or their students in order to exercise this art

---

[28] Original footnote: 11
[29] Strictly speaking, "duellists", also "sabre-rattlers".
[30] *d'avoir recours*
[31] *qualité*
[32] *murée*, lit: walled up

under penalty of 1,000 livre fine, "even of being proceeded against extraordinarily and of exemplary punishment if it should befall."

This police judgement was ratified by an injunction of Parliament dated 18 December 1759, which awarded half the fines to the Community of the Masters of Arms and the other half to the Hôtel-Dieu, less 30 livres for the costs incurred in investigating the infractions.

Louis XV expressly confirmed by his Letters Patent of the month of December 1758 the Statutes and Rules made by the Masters of Arms on 12 May 1644 and [they were] approved by the Châtelet[33] on 5 November following. The king had them registered in Parliament on 17 March 1759.

This same year, the Company had to make use of their rights in order to oblige the master of arms favoured[34] by the Duke of Bourgogne, Dalonneau de la Raye, to close a fencing hall which he opened in Paris.

Dalonneau de la Raye was not a member of the Community. Nevertheless, he thought himself sufficiently armed, thanks to a special warrant which he had been given on 6 August 1758 by the Count of Vauguyon.

But on 12 December 1759, an injunction from the provost of the Hôtel carried:

> That on the day of the notification of the said judgement, Dalonneau de la Raye will be required to close the fencing hall which he holds open and take down the arms and ensign placed by him at his place of residence. If not, he allows the Masters of Deeds of Arms of the King's Academies to take down the arms and ensign at the cost and expense of the said Dalonneau, forbidding him to take advantage in the future of the warrant obtained by him from Count de la Vauguyon.

This judgement was confirmed by an injunction of the Grand Council (23 August 1760).

The traditional ensign of the Masters of Arms belonging to the Community was an arm holding a sword.

We have a sign from a master *ferrailleur* from the middle of the 18th century.

It is a handwritten notice, embellished with two fencers, addressed as follows:

---

[33] This was in effect the police headquarters of Paris
[34] *privilégié*

Marteau, Master in Deeds of Arms
Student of M. de Liancour
Grand Court of the Temple

The Arsenal Library has an example of the Liancour treatise having belonged to Marteau.

The title "Master of Deeds of Arms of the King's Academies" came from those who taught their art in certain schools founded in the 17th century for the instruction of the nobility. These schools, placed under royal protection, carried the title of the King's Academies.[35]

On 11 April 1764, Parliament gave an injunction in the terms of which it was forbidden to all persons other than masters of arms received by masters exam or masterpiece,[36] to teach in the Colleges and Boarding Schools of the University of Paris, under pain of 300 livre fine and seizure of foils, plastrons, etc.

To avoid any surprise, the masters who were teaching were obliged to hand over to the Directors of Colleges and Boarding Schools a copy of their Letters of Mastery, certified by the Trustee and the *Gardes* of the Company.

The King's Academies ceased to exist one after the other. The Masters of Arms founded in 1788 in Danet's house, rue de Chantre, the Royal School of Arms[37]

Danet was the first director of this school and Teillagorry was deputy director.

Thus, we have arrived at modern times. The year 1789 will finish it.

For a long time already, the finances of France had been exhausted. At each meeting of the National Assembly, deputations came from all classes of society, in a generous spirit, bringing their offer to the Patria. The Masters of Arms of Paris are not the last. They presented themselves before the National Assembly, 17 in number, having at their head Teillagorry, then director of the Royal School of Arms, and Paquier, deputy director.

Here is the extract from the *Monitor* of 31 December 1789:

NATIONAL GAZETTE or UNIVERSAL MONITOR
(31 December 1789)

NATIONAL ASSEMBLY
Chairmanship of M. Desmeuniers

---

[35] Original footnote: 12
[36] *chef-d'oeuvre*
[37] Danet wrote a fencing treatise, published 1767, partly in response to Angelo, to assert French superiority in the smallsword.

A deputation of the body of the Masters of Arms of Paris was admitted to the bar.

Orator for the deputation: "The Masters of Arms of the Royal School of Arms of Paris come, as an example for all good Frenchmen, to present their patriotic tribute to the august assembly.

"Lords, intending to put the first weapons into the hands of French youth, our swords are the natural gift that we have to make to the country.

"Two metals compose them, silver and iron. Accept the first the for urgent needs of the moment. We swear to use the second in the service of the Nation, to maintain Liberty, to support your decrees and for the defence of the Good from kings.[38]"

The president to the deputation: "The sentiment of patriotism that all citizens show is a happy omen of the happiness which awaits us.

"The National Assembly receives with satisfaction the sacrifice that you make to the needs of the country and it allows you to attend the meeting."

Finally, on 17 March 1791, the National Assembly gave a decree ordering the suppression of all Corporations, Masteries and Guilds.

This decree put an end to the existence of the Company of the Masters of Deeds of Arms of Paris, two hundred and twenty-three years passing since its foundation.

Regarding the School on the rue du Chantre, which still rallied the members of the former Community driven by the fall of the monarchy, it existed only until 1792.

---

[38] *la defense du meilleur des Rois*

# Notes on the Historical Overview

### 1.

Here is the information that we have from the tax roll of 1292.

| | |
|---|---|
| Guillaume, rue d'Averon (today the rue Bailleul) | paid 16 sous. |
| Richart, rue de la Ferronnerie | – 9 – |
| Sanse, rue du Biau-bourg (rue Beaubourg). | – 2 – |
| Jacques, rue du Roi-de-Ceziie (rue du Roide-Sicile) | – 8 – |
| Mestre Thomas, rue de la Calendre .... | – 30 – |
| Nicolas, rue de la Buschorie | – 2 – |
| Phelippe, rue de la Serpante (rue Serpente) | – 12 deniers. |

### 2.

During the middles ages, one said *escrémie, esquermie,* etc for fencing[39] and *s'escrémir, s'escrémier,* etc in order to indicate the action of exercising in fencing, of combat or even disputing. The name of *escrémisséeur* was given to masters of arms. In an agreement between the weavers and dyers of the city of Paris, contracted in 1291, there is mention of Jacques *le scrémisséeur,* who added to his profession of master of arms that of weaver.

### 3.

Part of Paris, located on the left bank of the Seine and contained within the encircling walls built by Philippe-Auguste, is named the

---
[39] *escrime* in modern French

University. In this space are found enclosed colleges numbering forty-five in 1554.

The walls of Philippe-Auguste begin a little above the Pont Tournelle, between the current streets Fossés-Saint-Bernard and Cardinal-Lemoine.

The wall runs alongside this latter until the rue Clovis then, gaining rue Soufflot by rue de l'Estrapade, it crosses the Lycée Saint-Louis, the clinic of the School of Medicine, [and] Commercial Court in order to reach the Seine between the Hôtel de la Monnaie and the Institute.

### 4.

The suburbs Saint-Victor, Saint-Marceau and Saint-Jacques.

### 5.

In 1565, Catherine de Médici gave a splendid feast at Fontainebleau. Charles IX bouted before the Court with his fencing master, Pompée.

The Duke of Anjou, aged then 13 years, appeared afterwards. He fenced with his master named Silvie.

Catherine de Médicis had chosen these two masters, who were of her nationality, in order to give fencing lessons to her children. But in 1558 there was a french master of arms named Noél Carré who for four livres twelve sols per month taught his art to the pages of the stables of the queen mother.

### 6.

Henry de Sainct-Didier went on several campaigns, among others those in Piedmont (1554-1555).

In the composition of his work, he was certainly inspired by the principles of Italian fencing but he also expressed some personal theories, the fruit of thirty years practice.

Pierre du Fief was one of his best students.

Among the pieces of verse enclosed in Sainct-Didier's work in praise of the author, we noted a sonnet by Jean Emery, from Barre in Provence, and we give an extract of this sonnet because the word foil[40] is contained in the following verse:

---

[40] *fleuret*

*Approchas vous aucuns*
*Hou raco d'escrimaille*
*Quembe vostre flourès*
*Fasez ben pauc que vaille.*[41]

*Approchez-vous tous,*
*Race d'escrimailleurs*
*Qui de votre fleuret*
*Faites bien peu qui vaille.*[42]

Come ye all,
Race of fencers
Who with your foils
Do little of worth.

Here is the title of Sainct-Didier's book:

A tract containing the secrets of the first book on the sword alone, mother of all weapons, which are the sword and dagger, cape, targe, buckler, rondelle, two-handed sword, two swords, with figures having the weapons drawn in order to defend and attack at the same time the strikes that one can throw, both attacking and defending. Very useful and profitable for guiding the nobility and the followers of Mars according to the art, program and practice.

Composed by Henry de Sainct-Didier, Provençal gentleman.

Dedicated to the majesty of the very Christian king, Charles IX. At Paris, printed by Jean Mettayer and Matthurin Challenge and sold in Jean Dalier's shop on the Bridge of St Michael at the sign of the White Rose, 1573 with Royal Privilege.

Henry de Sainct-Didier, fearing counterfeiting of his treatise, took care to affix his signature on each copy below the advice to the reader inserted at the end. This advice is as follows:

Dear Reader, whoever among you would buy these books and find not the name, surname and titles of the author

---
[41] Original in Provençale
[42] Rendered into French by Daressy

written there in his hand, such books were not sold by his intention. In this case, he prays you bring them to him at his house and he will return the money that they cost you, [you] naming to him who sold them to you and, if you will do so much, take the author to him,[43] which will cost you nothing. Finally, the author will show you and explain the contents of them[44] which will cost you nothing in order to have recourse to justice opposing those who would sell such books and to please him.

When Henry de Sainct-Didier wrote his book, some works on fencing had already appeared in Spain, in Italy and in Germany. One had even been published in Anvers in 1538, a book printed in French but the author of this treatise is unknown. It is solely about the two-handed sword. We only mention it as a side note. Here is the title: *La Noble Science des Joueurs d'Espée* [The Noble Science of the Sword Players].

(On the front of the second sheet): "Here begins a good book containing the chivalrous science of the sword players in order to learn to play with the two-handed sword and other similar swords also with the hangers and other short knives which one uses in one hand."

(At the end): "Printed in the town of Anvers by me, Guillaume Vosterman, living at the Gold Hat, the year 1538, in quarto Gothique with 33 engravings on wood."

7.

In the reign of Charles IX, fencing was strongly in favour at Court. The king himself gave the example in engaging in this exercise in which he excelled as much as in tennis.[45] His brothers, the Dukes of Anjou and d'Alençon, were equally renown for their strength with the sword.

Among the great lords, the Duke of Guise enjoyed a grand reputation. At the demand of the king, Henry de Sainct-Didier bouted with the noble duke.

During the time of his quarrel with the Court, Henri de Guise lived at Joinville, near Vitry in Champagne. Wanting to appear in a tourney, the duke wrote to the Baron Sommièvre the following letter that we possess:

---

[43]ie: the seller
[44]ie:the books
[45]*jeu de la paume*

I pray you do not fail immediately on receiving this to come find me in this place with some good horses and your weapons because I am determined to fight on horseback and on foot and to run in the ring and have chosen you as one of the best men that I claim to have. From Joinville, 8 September 1571.

The Duke de Guise added in his own hand:

Sommièvre, I pray you do not fail and bring only one good horse and your most beautiful weapons.

Your best friend,

Duke de Guise

M. Sommièvre was named in 1578 bailiff of Vitry-le-François and captain of Vitry-le-Brûlé.

Politics embroiled the two friends: M. Sommièvre, who held the side of Henri III against the League, had to fight Duke de Guise in 1581.

### 8.

Vincent Vannarelli and not Banvarelle, thus the name is written in the injunction of Parliament of 12 August 1621.

Vannarelli lived on the rue du Sépulchre (now the rue du Dragon) and was a student of Hyéronime, master of arms of Louis XIII and of Gaston d'Orléans.

### 9.

Until 1644, the aspirant to the Mastery was tested on:

1. The sword alone
2. Sword and dagger
3. Halberd
4. Two-ended baton

In the new statutes that the masters of arms made in 1644, the examination only consisted of the sword alone, the sword and dagger and finally the two-handed sword[46] or sabre.

---

[46] *espadon*

Nonetheless, in order to show his skill, the candidate[47] made again some exercises with the halberd at first and followed by the two-ended baton.

In the 17th century, the aspirant only did a bout with the foil and another with the sword and dagger.

The test for aspirants to the Mastery was at first made publicly. One entered with tickets to the tennis court,[48] the place ordinarily chosen for this ceremony. But the crowd several times causing grave disorder, an injunction of 3 April 1759 constrained the number of master's assistants to the sons of masters and persons invited by the King's Procurer.

We give below a list which must have served as the program for the reception of Teillagorry the Nephew. We have respected the spelling of the names on our list which are handwritten. The reception of Teillagorry the Nephew must have taken place around 1760, for La Boëssière, the previous master received, was in 1759.

*Reception of Teillagorry, the Nephew. Names of the masters of deeds of arms of the King's Academies of Paris.*

1. M. Rousseau, Knight of Saint-Michel, Dean
2. M. Dumouchel
3. M. Daniel
4. M. Deladroit
5. M. Teillagorry
6. M. Fauveau
7. M. Leperche
8. M. Thonnard
9. M. Moter
10. M. Chabot +
11. M. Delarivière
12. M. Danet
13. M. Guillaume +
14. M. Donnadieu +
15. M. Delasalle +
16. M. Devaucour +
17. M. Delaboissiere +

The masters who bouted at the reception of Teillagorry are those whose names are marked with a cross.

---

[47] *récipiendaire*
[48] *jeu de paulme*

## 10.

In his memoirs, Brantôme said that in his time it was the fashion to go to learn to fence with certain renown Italian masters.

He cites among the most celebrated: Tappe of Milan, called the Great; Patenostrier of Rome, master of the sword alone, very excellent in this art; Hyéronime; Francisque; Julle of Milan; Flaman; Bartholomy of Urbin, master of arms in Rome.

He cites also Sir d'Aymard (of Bordeaux) who spent ten years in Italy, a gallant gentleman certainly, "when he lived," he added.

## 11.

Vincent Francquin or Francquin de Saint-Ange was born in Picinsco, a little town located in the Kingdom of Naples. Vincent de Saint-Ange migrated to France where he obtained letters of naturalisation (13 October 1617).

He was one of the signatories of the Statutes written by the Community in 1633 and in 1644.

He had the honour of being chosen in 1648 in order to give fencing lessons to King Louis XIV and received two thousand livres each year in order to fulfil this mission.

In 1652, he was named master of arms to the Duke of Anjou, brother of the king. The confirmation of Saint-Ange's nobility was registered by the Court of the Aides 8 July 1669.

Vincent de Saint-Ange, squire, knight of the Order of the King, drew his last breath on 26 March 1670 in a house on the rue Férou belonging to Louis de Saint-Ange, his eldest son, squire, aide-de-camp for the king's armies.

It is in the fencing hall of Vincent de Saint-Ange that in 1644 the bout of Philibert de la Touche with the celebrated Italian fencer, the Count of Dhona, took place.

In this bout, which made a lot of noise at the time [and which] de la Touche recounts in his fencing treatise, the Count of Dhona took the sword in the right hand and held the blade in the other hand around six or eight inches from the guard.

Philibert de la Touche gave him three clear hits, the number decided on for the bout.

*Patent of the King's Master Fencer at Arms*

Today, etc ... January 1648, the king being at Paris, having particular knowledge of the person of Vincent de Saint-Ange, his skill and value as a fencer, faithful and devoted in his service, His Majesty ... etc holds and retains him to teach fencing with weapons, at wages of two thousand livres each year, which will be paid to him henceforth and to come by the general treasury of his present household, for each year of his exercise. His Majesty wants and intends to that end, resting on the general state of the officers of his house of the said quality, that he enjoy the honours, authorities, prerogatives, pre-eminences and privileges belonging to that office without difficulty and by virtue of this patent he signed with his hand and countersigned by me, his adviser Secretary of State of his commandments.

*Patent for the Master Fencer of Arms to the Duke of Anjou*

Today, ... of the month of ... 1652. With the intention that His Majesty gives to the Duke of Anjou, his only brother, the masters that he will judge capable of teaching him exercises suitable to his person, he believes that for those [exercises] of arms he could not make a better choice than Sir Saint-Ange both for the reputation that he has acquired in this art through his experience and for the confidence that he has in his faithfulness.

This is why His Majesty held and retained in order to teach the Duke of Anjou to make exercises of weapons, wanting and intending that since he may be paid for the appointments that will be ordered by him for this effect in the estates that will by him be signed and stopped and that he will be employed in the capacity of Master of Arms of my said Lord in order to enjoy in this charge the honours, privileges and pre-eminences belonging to it as well as those that have been enjoyed and that have been honoured being similarly retained by virtue of this Patent that he has signed.

*Retinue of the Squire holding the Academy for the lord Saint-Ange*

From the King to the Grand Squire[49] of France and you treasurers and controllers of deeds and expenses of our stable, greetings.

The good services that our beloved Louis Franquin Saint-Ange, squire, Lord of Focux, gave us for several years as an aide-de-camp of our armies and the experience he gained in all the exercises needed for the instruction of the nobility, having resolved to honour him with the rank of squire holding an academy in our good city of Paris, for these causes, we have this day retained and retain hereby, signed by our hand, to the rank and duties[50] one of our squires into our academy of the said town of Paris for, by him, to exercise both in the said city as in other towns of our kingdom enjoying and using the honours, authorities, prerogatives, privileges, franchises, liberties, pledges, rights, income and emoluments [which] are accustomed and belong to such and similar as other squires enjoy holding academy in our said city and as we please. We command each of you that after the said Saint-Ange appears to you to be of good life, habits, Catholic, apostolic and Roman religion and the oath taken by him and received, as in such cases is required and accustomed, you will register this judgement in the records and papers of our said stables and enjoy and use fully and peacefully the contents of them and obey him and hear all those and any to whom it appertains things concerning this duty.

We command, moreover, the treasurers of our squires to pay wages to the said Saint-Ange in the future in the terms and in the accustomed manner following our estates, Because such is … etc.

Given at Versailles under the seal of our secretary 10th March 1673.

---

[49] Master of Horse
[50] *en l'estat et charge*

By another Letter given at Versailles (26 October 1675) a retainer for the squires holding an Academy in the city of Paris was given in favour of Louis Franquin de Saint-Ange, in place of lord Forestier[51]

Louis de Saint-Ange died in 1679. Godéfroid de Romans, squire, lord Nesmond, succeeded him in this capacity.

## 12.

At the start of the eighteenth century, there were three King's Academies in Paris.

One of these schools ceased to exist in 1760, another in 1769. As for the third, it survived until 1790, carrying the last title of the Royal School for Riding. The price of some fencing lessons was the same in the three Academies: each student paid eighteen livres per year.

When in 1760, the former Academy Guérinière (which became in 1752 the Academy Croissy) ceased to exist, the fencing master was Ladroit.

He had yet two years to complete the twenty years of practice required in order to be knighted.

Ladroit entered for survival the Academy Jouan. He remained from 1761-1765.

A little later, it was the same for Motet who lacked one year of completing his twenty years of exercise. Motet passed by the Academy Jouan which closed its doors. The Academy was led by Dugard.

---

[51] Original footnote: The Academy Forestier is noted on the map by Gomboust (1652) to the left in the rue de Sorbonne, now the rue de l'University

# Ordinances and Statutes of the Master Players and Sword Fencers of the City of Paris for the Regulation of the Said Fencing

(15 January 1567)

**Firstly**: that in order henceforth to protect the Art and Instruction in arms of the Master Players and Sword Fencers of the City of Paris, [we] establish two Guards of this Art, which will be [for] two entire years, of which one of the two will renew year-on-year. And the said Guards will swear before the King's Procurer to the faults and transgressions they find in the practice of fencing.[52]

**Item**: he who would succeed to the Mastery in the City of Paris will be required to serve one of the said Masters two years as Provost, otherwise called *Garde Salle*,[53] and, that time completed, will make the Provost General's prize play in order to have the liberty to frequent the halls of the other Masters. To this end, they having recognised the knowledge and the merit of the above mentioned, he will be tested by one or more other Provosts General if he is to achieve the said

---

[52] *au faict d'escrime*, in this context *faict* carries connotations of the reality, happening, occurrences, etc of fencing. The 'practice of fencing' seems a good compromise.

[53] a form of manager or administrator of the fencing hall

Provosty.[54] And the sons of Masters will be Provosts General without making a prize play or test.

**Item:** the said time ended in the case of he who has been a Provost who would aspire to the Mastery, he will be required to make a masterpiece, all the Masters being summoned in order [for him] to be tested by them in the presence of the Guards, and he will be required to undertake a prize play which will be observed and overseen by the said Guards, accompanied by a Master of the Art, who will serve him as Conductor in this place.

And the said masterpiece, well and duly made and the same being found sufficient, the Guards will be required inside twenty-four hours after the said masterpiece to make a report before the King's Procurer of the sufficiency of the same. And the Masters will make an Oath before the Procurer in such cases as is required and accustomed.

**Item:** the Guards will be required to visit the lodgings of the Masters in order to see and inspect their weapons, also to report in the Chamber of the King's Procurer the misdeeds and transgressions which they find in the practice of fencing.

And in the case that any of the Masters are found in contravention and that the batons and weapons are not found in good condition, the said batons and weapons will be broken and the Master condemned with a twenty *sous parisis*[55] fine, half payable to the king and the other half to the Guards.

**Item:** if any Master goes from life to death, the widow will be able to retain the fencing hall during her widowhood by means of a man knowing the said Art, who will be appointed by the Guards of the Art. And if she marries, she cannot take advantage of the privilege in that name.

No one in this City of Paris can hold a fencing hall nor act as a Master or call himself Master nor undertake to demonstrate the said Art in a Chamber or elsewhere, if he has not made a masterpiece and been tested as above. And in the case someone should be found contravening, he will pay a fine to the king of four *livre parisis* payable as above and their batons and weapons confiscated.

None of the said Masters can demonstrate or teach playing on the four solemn feasts of the year, the feast of Our Lady, [and] the feast of Saint Michael[56] on pain of twenty *sous parisis* payable as above,

---

[54] ie: the rank of provost, a member of the group of provosts

[55] Part of the complex pre-metric system of currency in which each *livre parisis* was made up of 25 *sous parisis*, each of which in turn was composed of 15 *deniers parisis*. All were silver coins.

[56] 29 September

because[57] Saint Michael's Day is the day of the Confraternity of the Master Sword Players.

**Item:** and because the Art in deeds of Fencing is of great importance and that it could come to varied misfortune through persons not tested who could have publicly received the grant[58] by virtue of Letters of Gift,[59] we want and it pleases us that the said Masters who will present themselves by virtue of the said Letters be tested by the Masters and Guards of the Art who will make their report of their sufficiency or insufficiency to the Justice, and where they are sufficient they will be received and not otherwise.

Signed:

Jean Coéfit,
Jean Langlois,
J. Goussu,
Mathieu de Lor

*Registered by the King's Procurer General, as it is contained in the Register of this Day at Paris in Parliament the 27 Day of January 1586.*

Signed: du Tillet

---

[57] *au moyen que*
[58] ie: of the title of Master
[59] *lesquelz se pourroient faire recevoir par vertu des Lettres de don*

# Ordinances of the Masters of Deeds of Arms of the City of Paris

(10 July 1633)

We, Masters of Deeds of Arms undersigned, see the abuses which happen daily in our Community concerning the reception of Masters who have been received against the injunctions of the Court and the former ordinances that we have on this subject. The principal cause of this disorder has only come from the too great a charity and accommodation by us all towards[60] those who have been presented to the Mastery, who have been preferred to the detriment and reputation of those who with pain and work have acquired this status, which must only be conferred on those judged, seeing its importance, by the *Jurés* and Elders as capable people and [as] those who know the misfortune which could occur.

    We, desiring to continue the former discipline that we had here in the past, have been advised to make an agreement together that we promise and swear to observe, point by point, even if previously we made some deviations, in order to endeavour to maintain for us that which nevertheless we had contravened.

    We have elected a perpetual Trustee to whom we give power and authority to enforce[61] this present agreement and ordinances. Submitting and obliging voluntarily to pay a fine of 12 *livre parisis* in the case that we fail in what we promise now, we give power to the said Trustee to constrain us by any means possible in the case we contravene it in any way and manner that may be.

---

[60] *à l'endroit de*
[61] *de faire observer*

FIRSTLY, we promise to observe an injunction of the Court of Parliament that we have against those who want to be received by Letters, holding they that will make a light test against six Masters and with four types of weapons.

That henceforth we cannot contract[62] any provost who is not native of the Kingdom of France and does not make profession of the Catholic religion, apostolic and Roman, and who is not of good character and good life. [He] will be bound six years in order to perfect himself and make himself capable of the Mastery. The said provost cannot carry the ordinary sword without having served his Master for the space of two years, asking leave of the Trustee and his said Master to wear it.

That he who will present himself for the Mastery will call the usual meeting in order to request a day, which cannot be made known to the applicant prior to the night before his reception nor can the selection of the place so as to overcome the disturbances which have happened before now. In our meetings, only Masters will enter. If anyone of the undersigned allows another to enter, he will pay the above fine for the first instance and for the second will be expelled from us and, being a rule-breaker, will no longer be called to any of our meetings.

That the prize for the receptions will be a silver sword for the first to the value of 18 *livres tournois*.[63] A gold ring for the second to the value of nine livres, a pair of deerskin gloves for the third to the value of six livres and a dozen sashes[64] of blended silver and silk for the fourth to the value of four and a half livres and that the dues of both the present and the absent will be put in common in the coffer of our Community with a note of that which was put there, except that our Trustee will have two *ecu*[65] and a pair of gloves of the value of 60 sols from him who will be received.

Before the oath is sworn, he who will be received will sign the original of our Ordinances and will pay[66] that which one is accustomed to pay for our confraternity and to support our Community.

If it happens in testing he who would be received that each strikes the other at the same time, it will be counted as null and they will recommence until the end of two clean hits[67] in order to prevent the

---

[62] *obliger*
[63] approximately 14 *livre parisis*, to maintain a common currency
[64] *esguilettes?*
[65] a gold coin worth three livres
[66] Original footnote: Editor's note: words erased from the parchment
[67] *bottes franches*

misuse that may occur.

After the usual test, if he that is to be received is deemed capable by the Trustee, *Jurés* and Elders, he will be presented by the said *Jurés* to the King's Procurer at the Châtelet to have him swear the accustomed Oath.

That if it happens that he is beaten cleanly by the first two, he will be sent again for a time that one will determine suitable to perfect himself, returning to him all the expenses he has paid out.

We promise to attend all advertised assemblies, finding us there on pain of an *ecu* for the first instance, if there is no legitimate cause such as illness, important business or absence obliging us to send our excuses. To default in doing this, the defaulter will pay the said fine from now on.

The *Jurés*, going to make the accustomed inspections, will have the power of directing those Masters who will seem good to them, if there is no legitimate excuse, to assist them, which they will do without giving favour to anyone.

If any provost wants to address any Master, the said Master will not be obliged to answer him, expecting unfairness.[68] Therefore, he will make his complaint to the Master of the provost, who will be obliged to present it before our Trustee and *Jurés* to receive such punishment which will please them to order. In addition, we forbid our said provosts to be assembled together in our rooms under pain of being chased from us and to be barred from the Mastery of arms.

That if any master quarrels or gives reason to quarrel in our assembly, the action will be condemned by the Trustee and *Jurés* as contravening our society. No one can aid[69] the offenders under the penalties carried by our said Ordinances. And in the case that the offenders want to attack our Trustee or *Jurés*, we are all bound to support him [the Trustee or *Juré*] and expel from us those who would try to corrupt our order.

That by common agreement, we will elect a Trustee who will have the coffer to our community and one key, who will present two notes about that which is found in the coffer signed by the said Trustee and the *Jurés*. One of which will be put in the said coffer and the other into the hands of the *Jurés* who will discharge the duty, who will hand over into the hands of their successors the two other keys, making their account of that with which they were charged.

And that the said *Jurés* cannot undertake anything concerning the business of our body without having communicated it to the Trustee,

---

[68] *attendu inégalité*
[69] *pourra assister*

the vote of whom will count for two and will have the power to compel those who offend our Ordinances and current agreement, as it is very plainly declared in the warrant which we have bestowed on him signed by us all.

That none of the undersigned can renew any past thing heretofore concerning misbehaviours occurring in the past in our Community so as to sustain from better to better our Society on the same pains declared in Article Eight.

We promise to observe and keep one rule that we have from the Bailiff of St-Germain-des-Pres that no one can teach our exercise in the said St-Germain unless he has been received and made an examination as we have.[70]

We will attend every year the service which is celebrated in the great Augustinian monastery [on] the day and feast of our patron St Michel under penalty of an *ecu* if there is not a legitimate excuse.

That henceforth the sons of Masters will be received to the mastery of arms, they making an examination against five or six masters like those who were apprenticed, and the said sons of masters will be favoured in that which concerns our dues in *deniers*[71] only and not other usual fees.

That if our Trustee, aided by the *Jurés* and four Masters of his choice, namely two elder and two younger, is compelled for the support of our Community to make such fees, both ordinary and extraordinary, they will be increased to that which they say without anyone being able to say to the contrary for whatever cause as may be.

In conclusion, we promise and swear to observe inviolably on our honour this current agreement in preference to and against all others. We submit again paying the twelve *livres* fine here above if we contravene it, of which Ordinances and current agreement each of the masters undersigned will have a copy signed by the Trustee and the present *Jurés* in order that no one can contravene claiming the cause of ignorance.

Made on this tenth day of July 1633 [by] Sir Langlois, valet of the wardrobe of the King's Chamber, being then the Trustee, and the *Jurés* Sirs du Rocher and de la Frenays.

Signed:

Langlois
de la Fontaine
de Riencourt

---

[70] *ainsi que nous*
[71] pennies?

Jacques Bourdon
Saint-André
Noble Henry
Jean Lecoq
Marres
Lavingne
Papillon
Bret de la Frenays
du Cornet
Vallet
Papillon
Langloys
Regnard
Alexandre Lemaire
Mory
Beaulieu
de Riencourt
Lescuier
Vincent de Saint-Ange
Du Rocher
Marc de la Roche
Anne Legoix

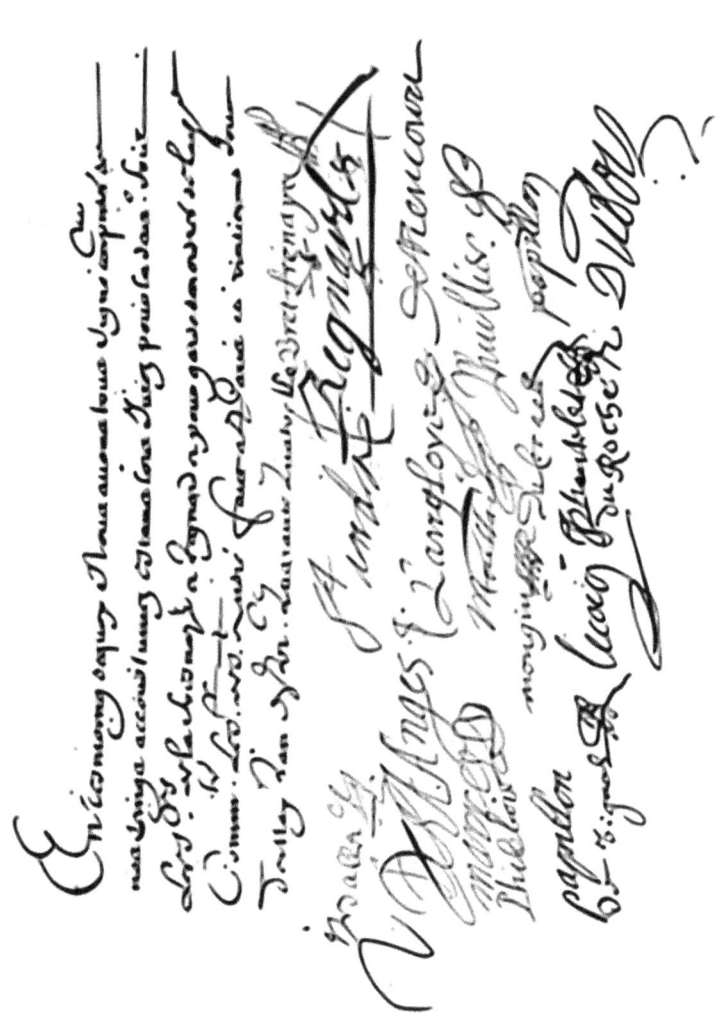

Signatures from the 1633 Ordinances

# Statutes and Rules made by the Masters of Deeds of Arms of the Town and Suburbs of Paris for the Support of their Privileges granted by Kings

(12 May 1644)

FIRSTLY, two *Jurés* will be selected by all the Masters assembled before Monsieur, the King's Procurer, at the Châtelet of Paris or in his hotel, and by the majority[72] of votes, in order to look after the business of the Community and do the necessary functions. The two *Jurés* will exercise the duty two entire years. And from there, within two years, every two years[73] a new election will be carried out of another two *Jurés* as above, without having regard to rank or order of reception but solely of persons capable of conducting the business of this Community.

---

[72] *pluralité*
[73] *en avant de deux ans en deux ans*

## 2.

On the day that the election of the said *Jurés* will be made, there will also be elected and chosen one of the masters, who will have previously been a *Juré*, as the Guards of the Order and Privileges to whom will be bestowed the coffer, moneys and all the papers of the said Community. For which coffer, there will be three different keys, of which two will be bestowed on the *Jurés* and the third will remain with the Guard, at whose house will be made all assemblies concerning the business of the Community during the two years that he is in charge. At the end of which, there will be another substituted in his place of the above said quality and will report jointly with *Jurés*, who will be examined by the general assembly which will be made to this effect and held closed and resolved by twelve Masters so that they do not meet further.[74]

## 3.

If a master of the Community desires to have and contract a Provost who could succeed to the Mastery, the said master will be obliged to go in person with the said Provost to the lodgings of the *Jurés* and Guard in order to certify to them that he who wants to be contracted is of good character[75] and good living, that he is of the Catholic religion, apostolic and Roman, of which he will furnish a baptismal certificate from the place where he was baptised, and a native of the kingdom of France, according to and in desire of the Privileges that he pledged to the King to give in favour of this Art as he is seen more fully by them.[76] That being verified by the said Master and a trustworthy respondent, the said Provost will be bound according to the style and form prescribed in the book of the Community, which for this effect will be brought by the said Guard to the place where the said Provost is, and the said Provost will pay 18 livres to the coffer of the Community, with the dues and gloves[77] to the *Jurés* and to its *Garde*, except the said Provost cannot carry the sword within two years after the passing of the said contract.

## 4.

That if any Provost removes himself from the service which he owes to his master, he will be reprimanded by the *Jurés* and the Guard

---

[74] *en cas qu'il ne s'y en rencontre davantage*
[75] *bonnes moeurs*
[76] *de donner en faveur de cet Art comme il se voit plus amplement par iceux*
[77] *les droicts et les gands*

at the first complaint that his said Master will make to them, which will be written in the book of the Community and signed by the said Master, *Jurés* and the Guard. At the second complaint, the said Provost will be let go from the Master and his apprenticeship[78] be ended and annulled before Monsieur, the King's Procurer, at the Châtelet. Any other Master that may be is forbidden from binding him and taking him for his Provost on pain of fine and annulling of the said apprenticeship certificate.[79]

And in order to stop the disorder caused by the liberty[80] that the Provosts take with their authority to make assemblies, both in the particular houses[81] as in the common halls of the said Masters, it is forbidden to the said Provosts to make such assemblies, except one lone Provost with the scholars of his Master who may go to the house of another Master in order to exercise themselves against the Provost of the said salle or its scholars. In case that another Provost had already entered before him, the said Provost will be in such a meeting obligated to retire himself or wait that the other may leave before he can enter there on pain of thirty livres penalty for the Master of the salle and the contravening Provost losing the time that he has already completed for the first instance that he will have contravened. And at the second instance, he will be let go from the Mastery of Arms and his apprenticeship certificate declared null.

5.

That any Master can only bind a single Provost at a time, not even taking one who may have been bound to another in order to achieve his time unless in the case of the death of the Master of the said Provost. In the case that any Provost abandons his said Master in order to "fight his campaign"[82] without his [Master's] consent in writing before a Notary, the said Provost will be excluded from the Mastery and in the case that he returns and that he obtains pardon from the said Master the time that he will have already done will not be counted and [he] obligates himself anew to the six years carried by the privileges of the Community.

---

[78] *brevet [d'apprentissage?]*
[79] *brevet d'apprentissage*
[80] *qui arrive de la liberté*
[81] *les maisons particulières*
[82] *pour battre son campagne*

## 6.

The time served by the bound being expired, and well and duly released by the Master of the Provost who will be presented to the Mastery, he will show again to the *Jurés* and the Guards of the Order his act of baptism in order to verify if he has achieved the age of 25 years, at which age he can be received if he is capable, and not otherwise. That being verified, his said Master will present him to the general assembly which will be convened for this aim and there his permission[83] examined and verified. The time will be ordained at which he can be examined, and advice given to the six Masters last received to hold themselves ready and in exercise for this effect. In case any of them is sick or absent, there will be elected another in his place in order to complete the said number of six, to whom will be given by the said aspirant the sum of twenty livres both to defray the expenses of the rooms and foils[84] that it will be convenient for them to have, in which rooms the *Jurés*, the Guard and two elders[85] will be conveyed in order to judge the two who will be the best in exercise in order to start the said examination when it will be ordered of them, without any others being able to gainsay them.

## 7.

The *Jurés*, Guard and the Master who will conduct the said aspirant to the Mastery will be obligated three or four days before that of the said examination to go to the lodgings of Monsieur, the King's Procurer, in order to know from him if he will be agreeable to convey himself to the place of the examination and to give the day and the hour of his convenience[86] to the *Jurés* and Guard alone, which will neither be revealed to the assembly nor to the said aspirant until the day before the said examination in order to avoid the disorder which can happen on such occasions and assemblies, in which only the Masters and sons of Masters and those who it will please the said lord King's Procurer will enter. And it is forbidden to all Masters of deeds of arms to allow entry to others on pain of twenty *livres parisis* fine payable half to the coffers[87] of the Community and the other to the poor or to pious works. Likewise, if any Master by neglect or otherwise is not found at the assembly[88] where he will be called for

---

[83] *brevet*
[84] *fleurets*
[85] *anciens*
[86] *commodité*
[87] *boeste*
[88] *ou autrement manque de se trouver aus assemblées*

the business of this Community, he will pay the said fine for the first instance in the case that he is absent or not sent his excuses. And the for the second, it will be declared to him that if he no longer wants to come, he will be excluded from being able hereafter to bind any Provost and will be enjoined by the *Jurés* and by the Guard to uphold the execution of the present article on pain of answering for it in their own and private names and of 100 *livres parisis* fine [payable] entirely to the poor and of annulment of the said obligation.

### 8.

The day preceding the said examination, the aspirant, conducted by his Master or others not participating in the bout[89] will go to the home of all the Masters of the Community in order to pray them to find themselves in the designated place for the examination, to await there Monsieur the King's Procurer. If any son of a Master having the age of 18 or 20 years capable of making an assault is found, the aspirant will undertake to bout[90] with them with sword alone and to give them each a pair of gloves of deerskin to the value of 60 *sols* each, and will deliver into the hands of the *Jurés* and the Guard the money that the other Masters gave on similar occasions which will be put in the coffer of the Community in order to support its affairs. Also, in this coffer will be entered half of all the dues owed to the Masters, except those of the *Jurés* and Guard conjointly with those of Monsieur the King's Procurer with the accustomed gloves, as it is carried by the order here attached, signed and approved[91] or as needs be.

### 9.

The aspirant will furnish two swords to the value of 25 livres each for the prizes which will be awarded to those who in the examination will strike closest to the heart, namely, one for sword alone and the other for sword and dagger. He who has earned the prize for sword alone cannot aspire to the prize for sword and dagger in order that the honour may shared by two. To maintain the Order, the Guard will undertake to carry the original of the said Statutes and Privileges and put them before Monsieur the King's Procurer, who will be entreated[92] by all the Masters to support the observance of

---

[89] *autre hors de rang de faire assaut*
[90] *sera tenu de faire avec eux*
[91] text has *omologué* which makes sense as *homologué*
[92] *supplié*

them. That done, the aspirant will be presented by his Master to the assembly of elders,[93] who will put him into the hands of the *Jurés* who will present him to Sir the King's Procurer and will name to him,[94] by their knowledge and by oath as needed,[95] two Masters of the six who must bout,[96] who will be the best in exercise in order to make the said examination without regard, as was said, to the order of their reception, in order to avoid all fraud and double-dealing.

### 10.

At the command given to start the examination by Monsieur the King's Procurer, or *Jurés* and elders in default of him, the aspirant will undertake to bout with three types of weapons against six Masters, as it was said, namely: with the longsword,[97] with the sword alone and with the sword and dagger. And for other weapons like the halberd and the baton with two ends[98] he will be exempted from them in the bout and will not use them before the assembly of the Masters in order only to make evident his skill. That if he is cleanly hit[99] with two strikes with the sword alone by the first who will examine him and that the second also hits him cleanly with two strikes, he will be sent on the spot again to school, and in the presence of my lord the King's Procurer, for a time that the *Jurés*, the Guard, the elders and all the assembly of Masters judge appropriate, without him having to repeat the costs that he will have made to this effect, except for the money that he is obligated to provide for the dues for his reception, which they will return to him immediately in giving the discharge that he will receive from the *Jurés*. That if in making the said examination, each struck the other in the same tempo,[100] it will be counted for nothing on both sides and [it] will be restarted and continued until one or other has given or received two clean hits.

### 11.

After the Provost has made the examination, if he is judged capable by all the Community, he will swear the oath before Monsieur the

---

[93] *l'assemblée des anciens*
[94] *luy nommeront*
[95] *si besoin est*
[96] *faire*
[97] *l'espadon*
[98] *le baston à deux bouts*
[99] *s'il est battu franc*
[100] *on se donne tous deux de même temps*

King's Procurer from the Châtelet and the day after will go, with his Master, to thank him for his assistance, likewise the *Jurés* and the Guard of the said Community.

## 12.

If any son of a Master desires to be received, he will show by his baptismal extract whether he has attained 22 years, at which time he can be received and not at a lower age. He will make the examination above, without hoping [for] favour unless in money only, except for the dues of the *Jurés* and of the Guard and of the accustomed gloves both to them as to all the Masters, and he will pay to the coffers of the Community that which the other sons of Masters have here above paid. And he will furnish the two swords of the same price each that the other Masters have furnished and he will give also the dues of Monsieur the King's Procurer and will swear the oath before him, if he is judged capable of the Mastery of the said Art.

## 13.

The widows of Masters will have neither any power nor privilege to have this Art taught after the deaths of their husbands and the Provosts who find themselves at the houses of the widows of the said deceased thus will retire themselves unto the *Jurés* and the Guard, who will support them to give to them another Master in order to achieve the time required by their apprenticeship certificate.[101]

*We omitted: that if the said Provost cannot find any Master who wants to take him, because all have Provosts, that it is lawful, in such a case, for any Masters who would want to have him to take him in order to complete his time. As it happened during the Jurande of Frenays and Regnard in the year 1645. M. Bonneau, being then the King's Procurer, gave a judgement that one named l'Isle completed his time with the first of the Masters which he desired, notwithstanding that he had a Provost. That which the* Jurés *here-above and the Guard agreed on 24 July of the said year 1645 in the name of the Community that such judgement, being just, must pass for law.*

## 14.

If any Master of the Art for private business,[102] illness or other accident is constrained to leave or abandon the Art and his salle, he

---
[101] *brevet d'apprentissage*
[102] *affaires particulières*

could, during the illness or accident (on condition that it not be for any bad action), have his salle and exercise the Art through his Provost, his son or, by the lack of the one or the other, by anyone capable of teaching. And when for private business outside of illness or other accident, the Master can absent himself and have his salle held, as was said, one year and three months only, at the end of which time, if he does not return in person to occupy the said places and teach the Art himself, the *Jurés* and the Guard will be obligated to close the salle and prevent any demonstration or any teaching there. That if it is for the exercising any Office which diminishes the nobility and dignity of the Art, he will be not only constrained to close the salle as swiftly as it will be allowed by that diminishing Office but also to renounce this profession except and unless it is [for] the privilege of some charge in the Households of the King, the Queen or the Infants of France.

### 15.

The above mentioned *Jurés* and the Guard will go before all the other Masters in assemblies concerning the business of the Community and will march and will give their voice according the order and seniority[103] of their reception and will have the power to conduct visits (which they should make from time to time in the service of the Community) to such Masters that they will judge appropriate, on pain of fine against the refusants.

### 16.

All of these Statutes and Articles here above, we Masters undersigned promise and swear to observe point by point without contravening them in any manner whatsoever. And we petition[104] Monsieur the King's Procurer to support us in them except in any cause or occasion that may be which could in any manner diminish[105] him.

In witness of which, we have all signed these present instruments[106] with our accustomed signs, being then *Jurés* of the said Art for the second time, the lords Frenays and Regnard, and for the *Garde de l'Ordre* of the Community, the lord Saint André. Made at Paris this twelfth day of May 1644. Thus signed:

---

[103] *ancienneté*
[104] *supplier*
[105] *desroger*
[106] *ces présentes*

Le Bret Frenays
Regnard
Saint André
Vincent Saint-Ange
Valet
De Riencourt
Langlois
du Roché
le Cocq
Marres
Moussard
Philebois
Papillon
Mongin
du Cornet
Lhuyllier
Papillon
Vignal

The said Statutes and Rules here above transcribed have been approved, this beseeching the King's Procurer, registered in the Register of the Audience of the Civil Chamber and Police of the Châtelet of Paris, by me undersigned, Dean of the Notaries[107] of the said Chamber, according to the judgement rendered by Monsieur the Civil Lieutenant, the fifth of November, made the said year and day here above.

Signed: Hubert

---

[107] *doyen des greffiers*

# Letters Patent

## (December 1567)

Charles, by the Grace of God King of France, to all present and to come, greetings.

We received humble petitioning from our beloved players and fencers with the sword in our town of Paris holding that on the 15th of January last they presented us a request which it pleases us to authorise and approve: the articles and statutes which concern their status,[108] here attached under the counter seal of our chancellor, drawn up by them for their regulation. We then sent this request to the Provost of Paris or his lieutenant, called our Procurer, in order to give and to send us advice on its contents in order to, having seen it, provide the supplicants with a judgement, which has been done and the advice sent to us, also here attached, and to the supplicants beseeching us very humbly to approve the said articles and statutes with our necessary letters.

We make known that after having heard in our council the requested articles and statutes, together with the advices attached thereto, as was said, on the advice of our council, in as much as we had touching and able to touch those statutes and articles authorised, confirmed, endorsed and approved, we confirm, endorse, want, authorise and it pleases us that they may undertake to keep and observe them without violating that which is contained in the said advice just as it has been made, conceded and granted by us.

We hereby give in commandment to our beloved and loyal people holding our court of Parliament at Paris, the Provost of the said place and his lieutenant and to all our other substitutes and officers to whom it pertains, that they read, publish and register the said present instruments together with the articles, statutes and advice, undertaking to

---
[108] *estât*

keep and observe point by point, according to their form and tenor.

We cease and make to cease all problems, impediments to the contrary, oppositions and appeals whatsoever and without prejudicing them, because we do not want them to be delayed, because such is our pleasure. And in order that this may be a thing certain[109] and stable forever, we have put our seal to these said present instruments without prejudicing our rights in other things and [those of] others in all.

Given at Paris in the month of December, the year of grace one thousand five hundred sixty-seven, the seventh of our reign.

Also signed on the fold[110] by the king in his council,

Charles

And to the side: *visa contentor*[111]

Thielement

And sealed on a ribbon of red and green silk, the grand seal in green wax.

*Registered by the King's Attorney General as it was contained in the register of this day. At Paris in Parliament the twenty-seventh day of January one thousand five hundred eighty-six.*

Signed: Du Tillet

Comparison was made with the original tendered.

## (December 1585)

HENRY,[112] by the Grace of God King of France and Poland to all present and to come, greetings.

Our dear and beloved masters of deeds of arms, by examination and masterworks in swordplay,[113] in this our good town of Paris, who have shown to us that King Charles, lately deceased, our very dear

---

[109] *fermé*

[110] *reply* – Cotgrave gives this as "The fould in the bottom of a Deed whereon we signe, and whereinto the labell is put for the seale"

[111] a formal legal term essentially meaning "registered"

[112] Henry III, b. 1551, d. 1589 (assassinated). King of the Polish-Lithuanian Commonwealth (1573). King of France (1574)

[113] *jeu de l'escrime*

lord and brother whom God absolve, by his letters patent in the form of a charter of the month of December one thousand five hundred sixty-seven had for the reasons contained there, confirmed, endorsed and approved the articles and statutes of the said status of fencing,[114] which they have thus undertaken to keep and observe, as they still do at present. But that some of the articles — even the second and the seventh, mentioning in said former, "whoever wants to attain to the said Mastery will undertake to serve one of the Masters two years only as Provost or *Garde-Salle*" and the said seventh "of the permission given to the widows of deceased masters, of making to hold the salle during their widowhood" — are defective and they have caused great inconvenience by the observation and undertaking of them, particularly the two-year time limit for standing Provost or *Garde-Salle* does not suffice in order to acquire the skill[115] required in this art which is of such consequence and importance, as all know, and, moreover, the said widows, under pretext of this permission, gave the teaching of sword play in their training halls to those who are neither Master nor well tested in the said art, and, moreover, they find those who makes a profession of demonstrating [it] in the suburbs and in some houses of the town without being masters by examination or masterwork.

In order to remedy [this], to cut out the evil which has come of it and avoid it in the future, requiring confirmation in other statutes of the said art, in amending the above said to command that those who would hereafter attain to the said Mastery will undertake to serve a master as provost or *Garde-Salle* for four years duration, that the widows of the masters, deceased and who will die, can no longer hold salle and that none can demonstrate the said art in the said town and suburbs if he is not master by examination and masterwork on the pains carried by the eighth of the said articles and statutes, that which the said petitioners[116] have very humbly beseeched and requested us to do both for the good instruction and conditioning of youth in the action of arms, the conservation of them, as for honour and reputation of the said masters and on that to make them dispatch our necessary letters.

We make known that we, considering these things, want to take heed of the above as a necessary and important thing after having been shown in our council the said statutes and the confirmation of them by our departed lord brother. From the advice of those and in our assured

---

[114] *dict estât du jeu d'escrime*
[115] *dextérité*
[116] *exposans?*

understanding,[117] full power and royal authority, we have confirmed and we confirm by these present letters the said former statutes and articles of the said art and play of fencing, except that which concerns the said second, seventh and eighth articles on which ones we declared and we declare that those who want to attain to the said mastery will undertake to serve as provost or *Garde-Salle* one of the Masters four years duration, that the widows of masters, deceased or who will die, may not hold salle nor demonstrate nor teach the said art in this said town and suburbs of Paris in salle or chamber if he is not a master by examination or masterwork and this on pain of one hundred *sols tournois* fine against each one contravening this, half payable to us, half to the Guards of the said art. Furthermore, we want the said articles, with this present declaration and confirmation, to be maintained, kept, followed and observed inviolably point by point according to their form and tenor in order to be enjoyed by the said supplicants as they have here before well and rightly enjoyed and used, enjoy and use still at present.

We hereby give in commandment to our loved and loyal people holding our court of parliament at Paris, Provost of the said place or his lieutenant and to all our other magistrates[118] and officers to whom it will appertain the content of this our present confirmation and reformation of the statutes of the said art and game of fencing to be read, published and registered and the content to be enjoyed and used [by] the said masters fully and peaceably. We obligate all those to whom it appertains to do, to suffer and to undertake this and in order to do this to compel by all means and manners rightly and reasonably notwithstanding any opposition and appeal whatsoever, and without prejudicing those not wanting to be deferred. Because such is our pleasure, notwithstanding whatsoever other ordinances, letters and things to the contrary, to those we have abolished and we abolish and to the abolishments of the abolitions contained therein.[119]

And in order that it may be a firm and stable thing forever, we have put our seal to these present letters, without prejudicing our rights in other things and those of others in all.

Given at Paris in the month of December, year of grace one thousand five hundred and eighty-five and twelfth of our reign.

---

[117] *nos certaine science*

[118] *justiciers*

[119] This is crazy legal-speak. Only an expert can decipher it. "*Car tel est nostre plaisir, nonobstan aussi quelconques autres ordonnances, lettres et choses à ce contraires, aux quelles nous avons dérogé et dérogeons et aux dérogatoires des dérogations y contenuz.*"

Henry

Thus signed on the fold for the King in his council: Potier

And on the side, *visa contentor*: Poussepin

Sealed on a ribbon on red and green silk in green wax with the great seal.

*Registered by the King's Procurer General as it is contained in the register of this day at Paris in parliament the twenty-seventh day of January one thousand five hundred and eighty-six.*

Signed: Du Tillet

Comparison has been made to the tendered original: Du Tillet

# (March 1635)

Louis,[120] by the Grace of God, King of France and Navarre to all present and future, greetings.

 We know how important it is for the security of our state, for military discipline and for the public peace that gentlemen and others of the yeoman rank[121] who want to make profession of arms receive the first precepts, instructions and skill for the handing of them from masters who are not only well experienced in deeds of arms but also who are of good living, morals and associated with the Catholic religion, apostolic and Roman, and well affectioned in our service. It is this which moved the kings our predecessors to make several statutes and ordinances to be kept and observed by the said masters, especially King Henry III, who by his letters patent in the form of a charter of the month of December 1585, reformed the former statutes and ordinances of the said art in order to avoid the great misfortunes which had happened from the liberty that the widows of the said masters had to have taught the said art and exercise of arms, and from that anyone can attain the said mastery after two years apprenticeship. He wanted and ordered that henceforth the said widows cannot teach the said art nor hold salle for this purpose, and that no one can attain the said mastery unless first and foremost he has served the said masters as Provost

---

[120] Louis XIII, b. 1601, d. 1643. Ruled as King of France from 1610 to 1643 and King of Navarre (as Louis II) from 1610 to 1620, when the kingdom of Navarre was merged with the kingdom of France

[121] *condition routière*

or *Garde-Salle* the space of four complete years and that he can only be received thereafter having made good and sufficient examination or masterwork and, that to the detriment of[122] one named Etienne Lasset, wanting to introduce himself into the Mastery without having served the said masters, making neither examination nor masterwork, by virtue of certain letters of mastery obtained by him. The said lord,[123] by his other letters patent of the month of June 1586, commanded that no one may be received master in the said art unless he has first and foremost made the said apprenticeship and [is] well tested. In that he could have obtained some letters of mastery by surprise or otherwise, together with all those that he could afterwards obtain, the said lord by his said letters broke, revoked and annulled that which is equally confirmed by other letters patent of the late king Henry the Great, our very honoured lord and father, of the month of December 1588. Also, by injunction of our court of Parliament of 12 August 1621, it was ordered that one named Banvarelle, granted letters of mastery in deeds of arms, would only be received after having made examination with six masters and four types of weapon. All the which observations we estimate all the more necessary and important that by means of them all those who will attain the said mastery will all be so clever and proven that we will have the greatest confidence in them for the instruction and education of those who want to know the profession of arms. Being formed by good example, good living, morals, association, faithfulness and affection in our service, the said masters will serve us with more capacity, affection and fidelity than if they have been appointed, instructed by foreign persons, of bad living and association, subjects or employed by princes, enemies of our crown, who could introduce themselves into the said mastery under the pretext of letters which were created for joyous events, births, marriages or naming of the Infants of France, and by this means making a great casual mixing[124] with the nobility and other people apt to carry arms in the middle of assemblies which happen daily at their houses, may by evil practices and means turn them from the service and faithfulness that they owe us. In the seeking of such letters, the said foreigners or other people not tested and of bad living render themselves all the more curious that in the midst of the great care, work and diligence of the masters at present exercising in our good town of Paris, the exercise and experience of arms achieving there such degree of perfection that whereas in the past, our subjects, accustomed to go into foreign

---

[122] *au préjudice de ce*
[123] ie: Henry III
[124] *une grande ordinaries fréquentation*

lands in order to learn there the said exercise and handling of weapons according to the foreigners, [they] are constrained to come to France for this aim.

For these reasons, in the example of our predecessors desiring to provide in this that such inconvenience cannot occur, we have had presented in our council the said letters and injunctions together [with] those given in favour of the master apothecaries, barbers, surgeons, goldsmiths, masters of moneys, furriers, milliners and writers by which the said arts and professions are exempted from the creation of the said letters of mastery, and considering their small importance concerning only the individual persons of our subjects. In regard to the said art and mastery in deeds of arms and swordplay which concerns the public peace, military discipline and preservation of our state, we have the advice of our said council and, by our special grace full of power and royal authority, said, ordered and declared, and we say, order and declare, desire and it pleases us that henceforth and always no one may demonstrate or teach the said art and exercise of arms and swordplay in this our kingdom and especially in our town and suburbs of Paris, in salle, chamber or otherwise if he is not a master by examination or masterwork, notwithstanding all letters of mastery for whatever reason or occasion which they may be or could have been created, either for joyous events, birth, marriage, naming of the Infants of France or otherwise, in whatever type or manner that may be, of a created donation, granting or succession which we have exempted. We exempt and reserve by these present letters the said art and mastery in deeds of arms and swordplay, in the same form and manner that the said master apothecaries, barbers, surgeons, goldsmiths, master of monies, furriers, milliners and writers are exempt and reserved, and where any of the said letters find themselves dispatched, by virtue of the edict here above made and those that by surprise or otherwise may be here after sent, even those sent in favour of the Title of the Duchess of Savoy, purchased[125] by our very dear and very loved sister, Christine of France, by our edict of the month of December one thousand six hundred and thirty-six. Wanting to support the said art and mastery of deeds of arms and swordplay in as much as needs to be, we have broken, revoked and annulled them and by these present letters we break, revoke and annul them. We rely on all our judges and officers to have regard to them all and to the said trustees, *jurés*, [and] masters of the said deeds of arms in receiving and admitting any to the said mastery by virtue of the said letters, on

---

[125] *acquis*

pain of cessation and nullification of the receptions and three thousand livres fine against those of the said trustees, *jurés* and masters who have preferred or processed their reception.

We hereby give in commandment to our beloved and faithful people holding our court of parliament at Paris, the Provost of the said place, bailiffs of the palace or their lieutenants and to all other magistrates[126] and officers to whom it appertains that they have to cause this our present declaration to be read, published and registered in the register of their courts and jurisdictions, undertaking to keep and observe them [ie: the statutes] inviolably, without suffering that they contravene them, compelling to make, to suffer and obey all those to whom it belongs by all right and reasonable means notwithstanding oppositions and appeals whatsoever for which we do not want it to be delayed because it is our pleasure. Notwithstanding also all ordinances, edicts, letters or other things generally whatsoever contrary to these present letters, to whom the contents may diminish, we have abolished and we abolish by these present letters signed by our hand. And in order that this may be a closed and stable thing forever, we have made to put and set our seal there, without prejudicing in other things our right and those of all others.

Given at Chantilly in the month of March the year of Grace one thousand six hundred and thirty-six.

Signed: Louis

And on the fold for the King: De Lomenie

*Registered by the Procurer General of the King in order to be executed according to their form and tenor, at Paris, in Parliament, the twenty-first day of January one thousand six hundred and thirty-six.*

Signed: Du Tillet

Comparison made to the original: Guyet

## (September 1643)

Louis[127] by the Grace of God King of France and Navarre. To all present and future, Greetings. We have received humble supplication

---
[126] *justiciers*
[127] Louis XIV, the Sun King came to the throne 14 May 1643

from our beloved *Jurés* and Master Fencers of our good town of Paris containing that the kings, our predecessors, recognising how important it is for the security of our state, for military discipline and for the public peace, that young gentlemen or others of yeoman rank[128] who want to make profession of arms, receive the first precepts, instructions and skill for their management from Masters who are not only tested in deeds of arms but also are of good living, morals, association, apostolic and Roman Catholic religion, and beloved in our service; having made several Statutes and Ordinances in order to be kept and observed by the said Masters; and, especially King Henry III, whom by his letters patent in the form of a charter of the month of December 1585 renewing the former Statutes and Ordinances of the said Art in order to avoid the great misfortunes which had happened from the liberty that the widows had in having the said Art and exercise of arms taught and in that all could attain to the Mastery after two years of apprenticeship. He ordered that henceforth the widows could not have the said Art taught nor hold salle for this end and no one could attain the said Mastery unless first and foremost he had served the Masters as Provost or *Garde-Salle* the space of four entire years and that he could only be received after having made a good and sufficient examination and masterwork. And in that one named Etienne Lasset, who wanted to introduce himself to the said Mastery without having served the said Masters, making neither examination nor masterwork, by virtue of certain Letters of Mastery obtained by him, the said Lord had said through his other Letters Patent of the month of June 1586 that no one would be received as Master to the said Art if he had not first and foremost made the said apprenticeship and been well tested. Any Letters of Mastery that may have been obtained by surprise or otherwise, together with all these that could be obtained after, he[129] broke, annulled and revoked. This was confirmed by other Letters Patent of the late King Henry the Great, of happy memory, of the month of December 1588. In consequence, our Court of Parliament of Paris, by the judgement of 12 August 1621, ordered that the one named Banvarelle, provided with Letters of Mastery in deeds of Arms, could only be received by them after having made examination with six Masters with four types of weapons. All these observations the late King Louis the Just, our very honoured Lord and Father whom God absolves, judged all the more necessary and important that, by means of these, all those who would attain to the said Mastery be undoubtedly able and tested and that one has a great confidence in them for

---

[128] *condition roturière*
[129] ie: Henry III

the instruction and education of those who would follow the profession of arms who, being formed by their good example, would serve with capability, affection and faithfulness; [and not] that if they be instructed and guided by persons not tested, of bad living and association, foreigners, subjects or employed by princes, enemies of our Crown, who could insinuate themselves into the said Mastery under the pretext of such Letters, the which they would seek especially; that in the midst of the great care, work and diligence of the Masters exercising in our good town of Paris, the experience of arms having come there to such degree of perfection, that instead of as in the past our subjects being accustomed to go into foreign lands in order to learn there the said exercise and handling of weapons, the foreigners are obliged to come to France for this effect. For this and other pressing considerations, after being represented to in his council with the said Letters and Judgements together [with] those given in favour of the Master Apothecaries, Barbers, Surgeons, Goldsmiths, Masters of Moneys, Furriers, Milliners, Writers, by which such Arts and Trades are exempted from the creation of the said Letters of Mastery and, considering the little importance of these which only concern the individual persons of our subjects, in regard to the said Art and Mastery in deeds of Arms, which concerns the public peace, military discipline and the preservation of the State, our said Lord and Father had by advice of his Council through his Letters Patent of the month of March 1635 similarly confirmed the said Statutes and Rules and ordered that no one can henceforth or ever demonstrate or teach the said Art and exercise of arms in this our Kingdom and especially in our town and suburbs of Paris, in chamber or salle, if they are not Master by examination or masterwork, notwithstanding all letters of Mastery for any cause or occasion that may or could be created, be it for joyous events, births, marriages, naming of the Infants of France or otherwise in any kind or manner that it may be, whether creation, gift, grant or concession by which the said Art and Mastery in deeds of Arms was exempted and reserved. And where any of the said Letters are found sent by virtue of Edicts and these, by surprise or as otherwise could be granted in the future – even those sent in favour in the name of the Duchess of Savoy acquired by our very dear and beloved Aunt Christine of France by Edict of the month of December 1633 which he did not want to take place – for the said Art and Mastery in deeds of Arms and in as much as is needed, these are broken, annulled and revoked and forbidden for all Judges and Officers to have any regard for them and to the said Trustees, *Jurés* and Masters in the said deeds of Arms to receive and admit any to the said Mastery by virtue of the said Letters on pain of cessation and nullification of the said receptions and of three thousand livres fine against those of the said Trustees, *Jurés* and Masters who had favoured or processed the said reception. In consequence of which, the people holding the Requests[130] of our Palace at Paris, have had by judgement of 18 July and 6 October 1642 condemned Jean Pillard, Master Fencer of Arms[131] of our Stables, who wanted to exercise the said arms in our town of Paris following the Letters and Warrants[132] obtained by him from our said late Lord and Father, 20 April 1637 and 12 January 1642, to close his salle with a prohibition against making any exercise outside of our said Stables and, on his refusal, ordered that the said salle be closed by one of the Ushers of the said Requests and the foils and other utensils of the said Pillard seized. And our great council by judgement of 30 June 1643, granting the opposition by the said supplicants to the confirmation[133] of other Letters of 2 November 1642 carrying confirmation of the said permission of exercising the said Art by the said Pillard and holding open salle in our town and suburbs of Paris, ordered that the above said judgements of the Requests of our Palace of Paris be executed according to their form and tenor and prohibited the said Pillard, aided by these Letters, to hold there or to open a salle in our town and suburbs of Paris. These Statutes and Rules, Injunctions and Judgements we esteem especially just and reasonable in that they are the true means of preserving the said Art in reputation, good estimation and the perfection to which the execution and observation of them have made it attain. Because the said supplicants, having very humbly petitioned us to grant the confirmation to them, we want them to be entirely observed. For these reasons, in the example of our predecessors, we desire to ensure that the above said misfortunes cannot happen and that nothing in any manner contravene the above said Statutes, Rules, Injunctions and Judgements. Having the advice of the Queen Regent, our very dear and very honoured Lady and Mother, of our council and of our special grace, full power and royal authority in confirming point by point the said Statutes, Rules, Injunctions, Judgements and Patents here above mentioned, we said, ordered and declared and we say, order and declare, want and it pleases us that henceforth and forever no one can demonstrate or teach the said Art and exercise of Arms in this our Kingdom and especially in

---

[130] A chamber of Parliament dealing with urgent causes and complaints addressed directly to the King
[131] *Maistre Tireur d'Armes*
[132] *Brevet de permission*
[133] *l'entérinement*

our town and suburbs of Paris, in salle, chamber or otherwise, if he has not, more than the said two years, served the said Master Fencers of Arms for four years as Provost or *Garde-Salle*, made examination or be Master by masterwork, notwithstanding all Letters of Mastery for any reason or occasion that may be, be it for joyous events, births, marriages, naming of the Infants of France, gift, gratification, recompense or otherwise in any type and manner that may be, creation, gift, grant and concession of which we have excepted and reserved through the present letters to the said Art and Mastery in deeds of Arms. Where other Letters are found sent or may be attained by surprise or otherwise, of whatever quality and type that they may be, we want them to have no place in the said Art and, inasmuch as needs may be, we have broken, annulled and revoked them, and by these present letters we break, annul and revoke them and forbid all our Judges and Officers of having any regard for them and to the said Trustees, *Jurés* and Masters of the said deeds of Arms, to receive them there or admit any into the said Mastery by virtue of the said Letters on pain of cessation and nullification of those receptions and of four thousand livres fine. So we give in commandment to our beloved and faithful the people holding our Court of Parliament, our Great Council, Provost of the said Paris, Bailiff of the Palace or their Lieutenants and to all our other *Justiciers* and Officers to whom it appertains that this present letter, our Declaration, they read, publish and register in the Registry of their courts and jurisdictions and this to undertake, to keep and to observe inviolably without suffering that it may be contravened, constraining all those to whom it appertains to suffer and obey by all rightful and reasonable means, against any opposition or appeal whatsoever. We do not want it to be delayed for it is our pleasure, notwithstanding also all other Ordinances, Edicts, Letters or other things generally contrary to this to which, and to the abolishments contained therein, we have there abolished and we abolish by these present letters signed by our hand. And in order that this be a closed and stable thing forever, we have thereto put and set our seal without prejudicing any other things in our right and in that of all others. Given at Paris in the month of September, year of Grace 1643 and the first of our reign.

Louis

For the King, the Queen Regent his Mother present

de Guenegaud

*Registered by the King's Procurer General in order to be executed and used*

Master of Arms of Paris Heraldry granted to the Company by King Louis XIV (May 1656)

*by the petitioners*[134] *for the aim and content of them according to their form and tenor, and as they have of them here above well and rightly used and employed, using and employing still in the present. At Paris in Parliament 14 December 1644.*

Du Tillet

## (May 1656)

Louis,[135] by the grace of God King of France and of Navarre: to all present and to come, greetings. Our dear and beloved Masters of Deeds of Arms, who are 25 in number in our good town, suburbs and surrounds of Paris, have very humbly reminded us that the kings,

---

[134] *les Impétrants*
[135] Louis XIV

our predecessors, with the aim of recognising the advantages that the security of the State meets in the employment of the said demonstrators,[136] the honour that military discipline receives from their skill, and the peace that the people have perpetually felt by means of their instruction, have prescribed them some Ordonnances and Statutes, even according several beautiful and great privileges which have been confirmed by us since our coronation[137] by our Letters Patent of the month of September of the year 1643, verified in our Parliament of Paris on 14 December following. But as virtue is always opposed and that their privileges gave [rise to] great jealousy, so daily some want to contest the status of their profession and the least capable, making comparison with them, despise them so strongly that they do not want to know them so that in execution of the verbal order of our Council, having seen the employment that they have until the present gloriously exercised in the Army, in the towns, in the country and everywhere where the occasion has called them – the warrants that we accorded them in order to show the exercises to us and our principal Officers; the public testimonies of Our Blood and all the Nobility for the advantages they have received for their Instruction – they have appealed in Our Council and demanded that which, having regard to the Ordinance of the kings, our predecessors, and Letters Patent of the month of September 1643, the said Petitioners and their Successors will have Letters from our Procurer in the Chatelet of Paris in which the merit of the said profession will be explained. The Trustees and *Gardes* in charge, and those who succeed to the Trusteeship and *Garderie* of the said profession after twenty years of actual exercise in our said town, suburbs and surrounds of Paris, counting from the day of their receptions, will carry the quality of Nobility, and [it] will be communicated to their descendants, without anyone being able to establish themselves in the extent of Our Kingdom unless he has been Provost under the said Exposants. Also to permit them that the Coat-of-Arms of their Community be of azure, two crossed swords, points high, accompanied by four fleur-de-lys, with the *timbre*[138] above the shield and trophies of arms all around. And [they] wil have some Gentlemen Academists[139] to their house in order to show them the exercises, as they have always done before, without the number of the said Petitioners exceeding twenty in the future.

---

[136] *Exposans*

[137] *notre avenement à la Courounne*

[138] An heraldic term encompassing all exterior ornaments including in this case the helm and mantling

[139] *Gentilshommes Academistes*

This Request [is] by Sentence of Our Council of the twenty-fifth of last August. We could have sent again[140] to Our Civil Lieutenant and Our Procurer at the said Châtelet for their advice on it, it being seen and reported in Our Council to be determined what is correct; in execution of which Judgement, the said Petitioners withdrew themselves to our said Civil Lieutenant and our Procurer at the said Châtelet, [who] gave their favourable advice in this meeting; in consequence of which the said Petitioners requested of us our Letters on these essentials. FOR THESE CAUSES, after having shown to Our Council the Ordinances and Statutes of the said Masters of Deed of Arms, together with the advice of Our Civil Lieutenant and Our Procurer at the Châtelet of 21 October 1654 under our counter seal, here attached, with the advice of Our Council, desiring to favourable treat the Petitioners, WE WANT that henceforth those who would be received as Masters in Deeds of Arms, having Letters from Our Procurer at the said Châtelet, in which may be mentioned the merit of their Profession and which the said Petitioners have tendered before Us, nominate between themselves, up to six in number, to whom We will accord Letters of Nobility for carrying into the future the quality of nobility after twenty years of actual exercise in our town counting from the day of their reception, which their descendants will enjoy. After the death of one of the six Masters, one will succeed in his place who will have the said time of twenty years of actual exercise from the day of his reception to whom We will accord the same Letters on the information which will be made on his life and morals without anyone being able to establish himself in our kingdom in order to make profession [of arms] unless they have been Provost under the said Masters of Paris. They will be required to show [their] Certificate again before the Royal Judges of the places where they want to establish themselves. Finally, we permit the said Company of the said Petitioners, by these present instruments signed by our hand, to take for their arms the field azure with two swords crossed points upward, the pommels, handles and crosses of gold, accompanied by four fleurs-de-lys with a *timbre* above the shield and surrounded by trophies of arms.[141] Likewise, to continue to have Gentlemen at their houses in order to show them the exercises conforming to the said advice that We want and intend to bring out to its full effect, without the said Petitioners being more than twenty in the future.

SO, WE GIVE IN COMMANDMENT to our loved and faithful councillors, the people holding our Court of Parliament, the Cham-

---

[140] *Nous aurions revoyé*
[141] This appears to be repeated text. Scribal error?

ber of Our Accounts and Court of Aides[142] at Paris, the Provost of our town or his Civil Lieutenant, and our other *Justiciers* to whom it appertains, that these present our Letters, they have them registered and to make, suffer and allow the said Masters in Deeds of Arms to use and employ the contents of them fully, peacefully and perpetually; ceasing and causing to cease all troubles and impediments to the contrary: FOR IT IS OUR PLEASURE. And in order that this be a closed and stable thing forever, we have had our seal put to these said present letters. Given at Paris in the month of May, the year of grace one thousand six hundred and fifty-six or of our reign the fourteenth.

Signed:

Louis

And on the fold for the King: Phelypeaux

And at the end of the said fold is written:

*Registered by the King's Procurer General in order to be executed according to its form and tenor with the restrictions carried by the Injunction of the Court. At Paris in Parliament the third day of September one thousand six hundred and sixty-four.*

Signed: Du Tillet

Comparison to the original by our Councillor Secretary of the King, Household, Crown of France and of its Finances.

## (December 1758)

*Carrying Confirmation of the Statutes of the Company of the Masters in Deeds of Arms of Paris*
(December 1758)

Louis,[143] by the Grace of God King of France and Navarre, to all present and to come, greetings. Our dear and beloved Masters of Deeds of Arms of the town, suburbs and surrounds of Paris have put before us that, being extremely interested on behalf of the public to prevent persons of poor morals being charged with the instruction of youth and principally of the nobility, they have always ensured with

---

[142]*Cour des Aydes*
[143]Louis XV (15 Feb 1710 – 10 May 1774, ruled from 1 Sept 1715, succeeding his father at age 5, until his death. Known as *le Bien Aimé*, "the Beloved"

care to only receive amongst them persons of irreproachable conduct and they have rejected likewise all those suspect persons wanting to set themselves up as masters of their Art. That some abuse were introduced in the sixteenth century, they have righted in order to repair them in a Rule in the form of Statutes, 15 January 1586, whose the execution has been commanded, which had as its aim the election of *Jurés*, Provosts of Masters, the discipline which they must observe and the reception of Aspirants. But, it not having sufficed to stop all the disorders, they addressed these anew on 12 May 1644. The wisdom of these Statutes having been recognised by the Châtelet, they were approved without difficulty by the Judgement of 5 November of the same year. But even though the petitioners, having always brought the most scrupulous attention to the execution of them, nonetheless as some seek to oppose that which we have expressly confirmed, they see they must have recourse to our authority, supplicating us very humbly to accord them our Letters Patent on these necessities. FOR THESE REASONS, and desiring to assist the laudable intentions of the petitioners, with the advice of our council, which has seen printed the said Statutes here attached under the counter seal of our Chancellery and with our special grace, full power and royal authority, we have approved, confirmed and authorised, and by these present letters signed by our hand, we approve, confirm and authorise the said Articles, Statutes and Rules of 12 May 1644. We want and it pleases us that they be kept and observed according to their form and tenor, and without any contravention under the pains carried here. SO WE GIVE IN COMMANDMENT to our loved and faithful Councillors, the people holding our Court of Parliament at Paris, and our other Officers to whom it appertains, that these present letters be registered and the said Masters in Deed of Arms, present and to come, make use and employ the contents of them, fully, peacefully and perpetually, ceasing and making to cease all troubles and impediments, notwithstanding all things to the contrary: FOR IT IS OUR PLEASURE. And in order that this may be a closed and stable thing forever, we have had our seal put to these said present letters. Given at Versailles in the month of December, the year of grace one thousand seven hundred fifty-eight and of our reign the forty-fourth.


Signed:

Louis

For the King: Phelypeaux

*Registered, seen by the King's Procurer General for use by the said beneficiaries and their successors with the effect and contents of them and to be executed according to their form and tenor following the Judgement of this day.*

Signed: Dufranc

# Judgement Against Vincent Banvarelle

*Which ordered that Vincent Banvarelle, furnished by the Queen with Letters of Mastery, may only be received as Master Fencer after having made a light examination.*

(12 August 1621)

    Between the Master *Jurés* in deed of arms of this town of Paris, appealing the injunctions and judgements rendered by the bailiff of St Germain de Pres or his lieutenant on the tenth and eighteenth of July one thousand six hundred and nineteen, advice rendered by the substitute of the King's Procurer General at the Châtelet on the twenty-first of August one thousand six hundred and twenty, the judgement of the Provost of Paris or his civil lieutenant confirming the said advice on the twenty-second of the said month of August, etc, notwithstanding the appeal given by the same judge on the third of September of the said year, reception by the said substitute of the King's Procurer General at the Châtelet on the fifth of the same month and year in the person of the appellant[144] for the masters in deeds of arms in this town of Paris [who] undertook an examination, together with another act of reception since made by the said bailiff of St Germain or his lieutenant on the 14 December and following in the said year six hundred twenty of the one on the one hand, and Vincent Banvarelle so-called,[145] furnished by letters of mastery in deeds of arms in this town of Paris, defendant, on the other, without the qualifications being prejudicial for the Master *Jurés* of Arms according to Langlois and Le Féron for the appellant being called out.

    Regarding the advice of the substitute of the King's Procurer Gen-

---

[144] *intimé*
[145] *soi-disans*

eral of the Châtelet and that of the Civil Lieutenant and the judgement of the Bailiff of St Germain, by which they have commanded that the defendant would be received master without making any examination against the statute and an injunction given in similar cause in the year one thousand six hundred and one, Langlois concluded that it may be said to have been badly judged. [Langlois] asks that before he is received he undertakes an examination, be it great or small. And Le Féron, on the contrary, that the capacity of the defendant is sufficiently recognised by being a student having served Hiéronyme[146] who demonstrated to the King, to monsieur his brother, also that conforming to the edict of the creation of the mastery which carries that all the masters will be received without making examination being carrier of letters that the Queen freely gave to him supporting that he has been very well judged. Servin, for the King's Procurer General, said that he should follow the rule carried by the injunction of the year one thousand six hundred and one. And as much as the Provost of Paris pronounced, without drawing in consequence requiring a prohibition to be made by him of employing the pronouncement of the Court, [he] has put and puts the appeal to nothing without fine, has commanded and commands that the defendant will be received master fencer of arms by making a light examination with six masters and four types of weapon in the presence of the masters René le Roullier and Jacques le Cagneax, King's councillors, and having regard to conclusions of the King's Procurer General, having made and making to inhibit and forbid the Provost of Paris of further pronouncing without drawing any consequence.

---

[146] Cavalcabo?

# Judgements Against the Master of Arms Called *Ferrailleurs*

## (18 December 1685)

*Extract from the Register of the Chamber of Monsieur the King's Procurer*

Judgement rendered to the benefit of the Trustees, Masters and Guards of the Company of the Masters in Deeds of Arms of Paris forbidding one named Bary, *ferailleur*, defendant, of intruding himself into the exercise of the Masters of arms and commanding the closure of the salle where he teaches the said art.

Between Master Denis le Redde, attorney,[147] and René Thomas, squire, lord of the Chapel, Trustee, François Chardon and Louis Filleul, Masters and Guards of the Company of Masters in Deeds of Arms, petitioners, at the end of their exploits of the fifth of the present month by Jacquemin, Sergeant at the Châtelet,[148] directed on the 8 of the present month by Rielle on the one hand – and Bary, *ferailleur*, having been found demonstrating the exercise in deeds of arms, foil in hand, socks and sandals on the feet, defendant and at fault on the other hand. Le Redde in his pleading and following from the judgement given against Bary, neither [him] nor anyone else appearing for him, read the statutes and rules of the Community of the Masters in Deeds of Arms; the judgements and rules of the Police date 18 May 1640 and 18 November 1653 by which it is forbidden to all persons to intrude themselves in the deeds of arms to demonstrate or teach in public, be it in salle, chamber or college or other place of

---

[147] *procurator*
[148] *sergent à verge*

the town and suburbs of Paris, if they have not received Masters in Deeds of Arms on pain of confiscation of the plastrons, foils and other things with which will be found and one hundred *livres parisis* fine for the first time applied, half to the community of the said masters of arms and the other half to the Hôtel Dieu; of the confirming injunctions of the said judgements dated 6 February 1666 and 21 May 1667; of the deed of the petition above dated. We have forbidden and [we] forbid the said Bary of intruding himself in the exercise of the master of arms. We forbid him of further relapsing[149] on greater fine and confiscation of foils and other things on which he will be found relying in the said exercise in master of deeds of arms and will close the salle and further we command that the statutes and rules, judgements and injunctions will be executed according to their form and tenor. We condemn the defendant to pay fees of three livres not including the present and let it be signified.

Made by Monsieur the King's Procurer

Signed: Rocard

## (18 December 1685)

Two other judgements of the same type and in the same terms are rendered on the same day against:

| | |
|---|---|
| Lhoste, | |
| Caudat | *ferrailleur* |

## (23 June 1724)

Judgement of the Police forbidding all masters in deeds of arms without rank, called *ferrailleurs*, of making any exercise of the said art.

    2nd – To all proprietors and principal lessees of renting to them any salle.

    3rd – And to all wine or beer merchants of suffering them at their house.

---

[149] *récidiver*

# (14 June 1765)

| Dumesnil, | |
| Delafosse | *ferrailleur* |

Sentenced in absentia[150] with damages and the rooms where they exercised closed and walled for six months.

## Court Injunctions Concerning Colleges and Boarding Houses

*Extracts of the register of Parliament of 19 December 1763 and 11 April 1764.*

LOUIS[151] by the Grace of God, etc ...

In consequence, forbidding all persons, of whatever quality and condition they may be, other than Master in Deeds of Arms by examination or masterwork, from teaching the Art and Exercise of Arm in the town, suburbs and surrounds of Paris, and notably in the Colleges and Boarding Houses attached to the University of Paris, on pain of three hundred livres fine, payable by each of the contraveners and the confiscation of the foils, plastrons and other tools of the said Art. Similarly, forbidding the Superiors of the said Colleges and Boarding Houses to allow to enter the said Colleges and Boarding Houses any persons without quality in order to teach the said Art and to suffer that they give lessons on the said Art to their scholars. And in order to avoid all surprises, ordering that the Masters who will be received in order to give lessons in the said Colleges and Boarding Houses will undertake to give the Superiors of the said Houses one copy of their Letters of Mastery certified by the said Masters of Arms, etc.

---

[150] *Condamnés par defaut.* Cotgrave notes "want of appearance before a Iudge"
[151] Louis XV

# Masters of Arms of Paris (1556-1850)

The list which we publish includes the majority of the masters of arms who have taught their art in the city of Paris. This list, which starts in the middle of the sixteenth century, finishes with the year 1850.

We have inscribed the names of the masters of arms and the addresses of some among them in chronological order according to the documents that we have consulted.

These dates, addresses and names were revealed to us, not only in the address books, in the Almanacs of Paris, of Versailles, etc, but also in a certain number of original pieces that we possess or which have been communicated to us.

We have rectified the errors that we could discover. To cite an example, the Almanac Royal, from 1789-1792, carries Danet as director of the Royal School of Arms and Teillagorry as deputy director.

An official document allows us to state that 31 December 1789, when the Masters of Arms of Paris went in deputation to the National Assembly, Teillagorry was the Director of this School and Pâquier the deputy director.

Certain streets of Paris were given as donations to Masters of Arms. Several of these streets no longer exist.

While appreciating the marvellous transformations that have made Paris the queen of capitals, we could not prevent – we who are Parisian – feeling a sense of regret in following with the eye the wide gaps made by the picks of the demolishers.

It seems to us [we are] watching disappear the legends of the Paris of former times, legends both native and terrible, sometimes mysterious, often also full of amorous poetry, but in all cases legends attractive and always instructive.

How often we have sunk into the old lanes, penetrated the houses, foraging with a scrutinizing eye the be-greened stone courtyards in the hope, too often disappointed, of discovering some vestige of a monument of another age!

But also, how often have we been stopped in the course of our investigations by the faithful guardian of the property for having neglected the sign "speak to the gatekeeper," replacing the "beware of the dog" of ancient times!

We ask the reader's pardon for this digression and we return to our subject.

We will note on the side of the street names which no longer exist the former placement of these streets in relation to the new byways.

Many streets having changed name, we will add to the names which they carry today those which previously designated them.

Several masters of arms lived in the rue du Chantre and rue des Boucheries-Saint-Germain, which have both disappeared. The rue des Boucheries, which is carried by the Boulevard Saint-Germain, started at the Carrefour de l'Odéon, crossed the street now named Grégoire-de-Tours and came to an end between the rue du Four and rue de Buci.

The rue du Chantre started at the rue de Beauvais, near the Place du Louvre and finished at rue Saint-Honoré, nearly face-to-face with the rue des Bons-Enfants. The building of the new Louvre, the rue de Rivoli and the apartments of the Magasins du Louvre have absorbed entirely the rue du Chantre.

# Archives of the Masters of Arms of Paris

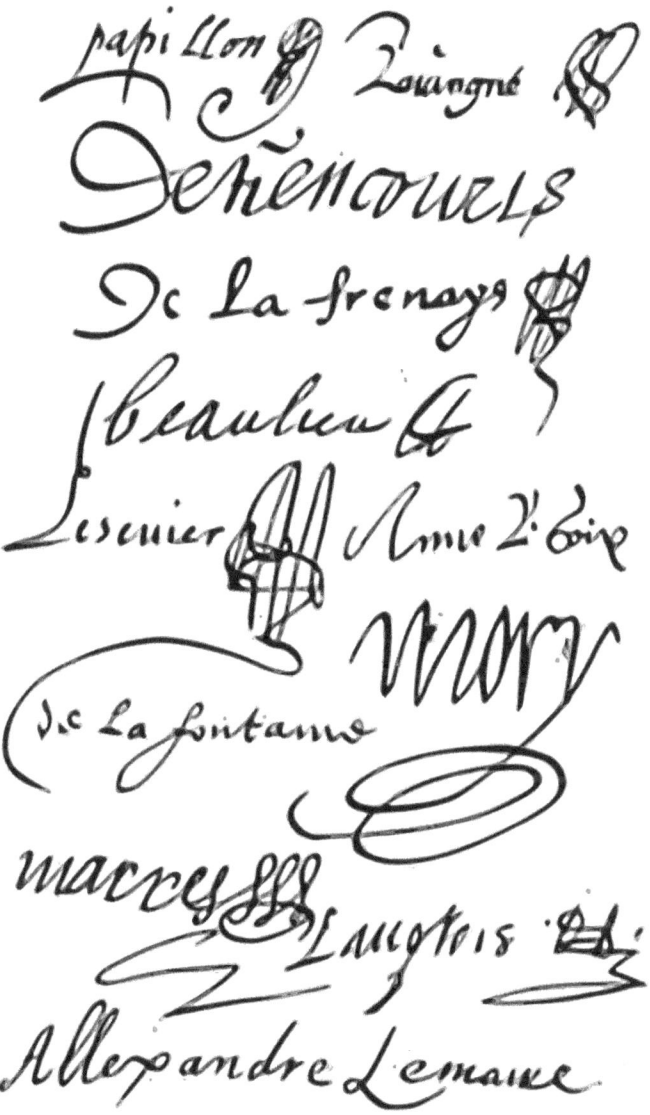

Signatures from the 1633 Statutes

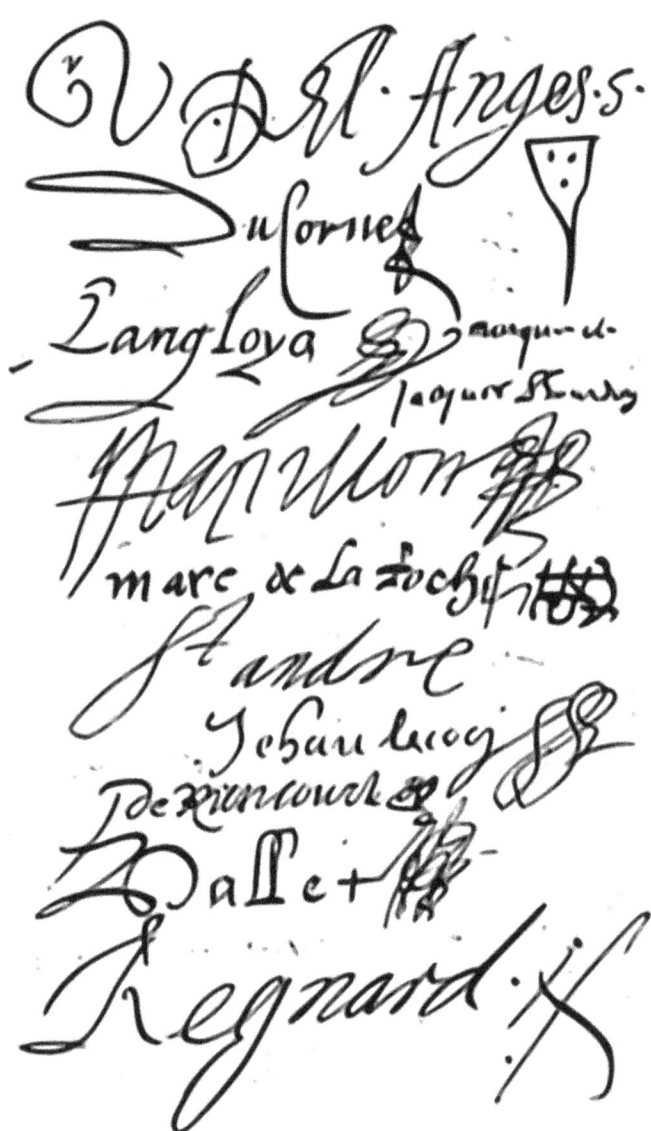

Signatures from the 1633 Statutes

## List of the Masters of Arms

Gossu or Goussu (Mathieu), rue de la Vieille-Pelleierie, 1556

Gossu or Goussu, junior (Jehan), rue de la Boucherie, 1556. He was one of the signatories of the Statutes of 1567.

Carré (Noël), master of arms to the pages of the stables of Catherine de Médici, 1558

Pompée, taught fencing to Charles IX, 1565

Silvir, master of arms of the Duke of Anjou (Henri III), 1565

Coéfit (Jean), 1567

Langlois (Jean), 1567

De Lor (Mathieu), 1567, rue Saint-Jacques, 1570

Musquin (Egard), 1586

Cochey (C), 1587

Duc (Marcel), 1587

Grandjean, 1587

Langlois fils (Jean), 1587

Vallet (Pierre), 1587

Laloy, 1587

De Riquebourg (Sébastien), 1587

Prévôt (Alexandre), 1587

Petit (P.), 1587

Petit fils (Jean), 1587

Papillon (Gérard), 1587-1633

Belly (Marcel), 1587

Chaudière (Pierre), 1588

Lecoq (Jean), 1589

Charreny (Pierre), 1589

Dubuisson (Nicolas), 1590

Charpentier (Claude), 1590

Dubuisson (Marcel), 1594

Bourdon (Jacques), 1604-1633

Hiéronyme (Cavalcabo?), master of arms of Louis XIII et of Gaston d'Orléans, brother of the king.

Cavalcabo (César) master fencer at arms of the Court, 1611-1642. He received 300 livres per year.

Langlois, trustee in 1633. He was Valet of the Wardrobe of the King's Chamber.

Du Rocher or du Roché, *juré* in 1633. 1633-1644

Bret de la Frenays, 1633. This master signed also Le Bret-Frenays (1644), *juré* in 1633, in 1644 and in 1645.

Vallet (Pierre), 1633-1644

Pillard, (Jean) master of the pages of the King's Stables, 1637.

De la Fontaine, 1633

De Riencourt, 1633

De Riencourt, 1633-1644

Noble (Henry), 1633. We have omitted his signature in the facsimile.

De Saint-Ange (Vincent Franquin) master of arms of Louis XIV and of the Duke of Anjou, brother of the king, 1633-1670

De Saint-Andre, *Garde de l'Ordre* of the Community in 1644. 1633-1644

Marres, 1633-1644

Du Cornet (Hubert), native of Liège, was naturalized French. 1633-1644

Regnard, *juré* for the third time in 1645, was ennobled in 1657. 1633-1657

Beaulieu, 1633

Legoix (Anne), 1633

Mory, 1633

Lavingne, 1633

Lemaire (Alexandre), 1633

Lescuier, 1633

De la Roche (Marc), 1633

Philebois, 1633

Vignal, 1633

Lecoq (Jehan or Jean), signed also as Lecocq, master of arms of the pages of the King's Grand Stable, was ennobled in 1657. He died in 1670. 1633-1670.

Papillon, 1633-1644

Langloys, 1633-1644

Moussard, 1644

Mangin, 1644

Prantebert (?)[152] 1644

Lhuillier, 1644

Papillon the younger, 1644

Dubois, 1644

De la Touche (Philibert M., sir) master of arms of the Queen's Pages and of the Pages of the Chamber of the Duke of Orléans. De la Touche is the author of a fencing treatise which appeared in 1670. 1644-1670.

De l'Isle (Denis-Beneton) was in 1652 master of arms of the Pages of Mademoiselle de Montpensier, daughter of the Duke of Orléans. De l'Isle received 200 livres per year. In 1670, he was *Garde de l'Ordre* of the Community for the second time. On 22 January 1685, De l'Isle was named master of the pages of the King's Little Stable, replacing Pierre des Fontaines.

De la Chapelle (René-Thomas) master of the pages of the Household of Mademoiselle (1661-1676). He received 400 livres per year. Thomas de la Chapelle was trustee of the Community n 1670, in 1683 and in 1685.

Langlois (Pierre) master of arms of the King's Household, 1664-1688

Marais, former trustee, 1670

Mangin-Galland had been twice *Garde de l'Ordre* before 1670

Soret, former master, 1670

De Lorme, former master, 1670

Héron, former master, 1670

---

[152] Original footnote: Signature unreadable on the original piece

Morint, former *Garde de l'Ordre*, 1670

Filleul (Louis) former master in 1670, was elected *Garde de l'Ordre* in 1685

Fargeot, 1670

Chardon (François) *Garde de l'Ordre* in 1685, lived in 1692 on the rue de Buci. 1670-1692

Rousseau (Pascal) Knight of the Order of the King. He was, after Saint-Ange, the master of arms to Louis XIV. Rousseau lived on the rue de Seine. He died there on 9 August 1688. 1670-1688.

Rousseau (Jean) was named 27 April 1670 master of arms of the pages of the King's Grand Stable, replacing Jean Lecoq, deceased. Rousseau was named in 1684 master of the pages of the Little Stable in place of Pierre des Fontaines, resigned. Later, he was chosen to teach fencing to the Duke of Bourgogne. 1670-1692.

Mongin the younger, 1670

Le Perche (Jean-Baptiste) published a treatise of fencing in 1676, 1670-1692. Rue de la Harpe in 1692.

Petit (Pierre) master of the little stable of the king, resigned in 1676

Des Fontaines (Pierre) 11 January 1676 he was named master of arms of the Little Stable, replacing Pierre Petit, resigned. Des Fontaines resigned in 1684.

De Saint-André junior, *Garde de l'Ordre* of the Community in 1683, living in 1692 on the Quai des Augustins.

Dubois, *Garde de l'Ordres* in 1683 and in 1685. His house was in 1692 on the rue Mazarine near the Metz *jeu de paume*[153] (this *jeu* was situated in the Commerce courtyard next to the rue Saint-André-des-Arts).

Dujon de la Salle (Fabien-Etienne), 1690

De Liancour (Wernesson) is the author of a treatise which appeared in 1686. In 1716, he was trustee of the Company for the third time. He lived in 1692 in the rue de la Boucheries-Saint-Germain and died in 1732.

De Brye (J.) He was in the rue de Buci in 1692 and published a fencing treatise in 1721.[154]

---

[153] tennis or handball court?
[154] *The Art of Fencing* [*L'Art de Tirer des Armes Reduit en Abrégé Méthodique*], translated

Pillard senior, rue Dauphine, 1692

Minoux, rue des Mauvais-Garçons (now rue Grégoire-de-Tours, 1692)

Le Perche elder, rue Mazarine, 1692-1729

Du Fay or Dufays, rue du Chantre, 1692

Pillard junior, rue des Cordiers (1692). Rue Mazarine (1725-1742).

Bourdet de Vaux (Nicolas) master of the pages of the Household of the Duke of Berry. 1711-1714. He received 200 livres per year.

Rousseau (Henri-François), master of arms to Louis XV, *Garde de l'Ordre* in 1716. He died in the rue de la Sourdière 18 May 1756.

Lebrun, *Garde de l'Ordres* in 1716 and in 1738

Le Perche *cadet*, rue des Boucheries-Saint-Germain, 1725-1739

Desfossez, rue d'Anjou (rue de Nesles), near the rue Dauphine from 1725 to 1729. Rue de la Comédie-Française (1729-1733).

Dumouchel, trustee of the Company in 1738. Rue Mazarine, opposite the rue Guénégaud (1729-1733). Near the rue de la Comédie-Française (rue de l'Ancienne Comédie, 1733-1751). Rue Saint-Martin (1760).

Landon was *Garde de l'Ordres* in 1738

Teillagorry (Bertrand), trustee around 1752, *Garde de l'Ordre* in 1759, master of arms of the stables of the Duke d'Orleans 1738-1767. His wife owned a house on the rue Neuve-des-Petits-Champs in 1750.

Rousseau, son of Henri-François Rousseau, had the title master of arms to the Infants of France and gave fencing lessons to the Dauphin, son of Louis XV. Rousseau received the Order of Saint-Michel in 1754 and was ennobled the year following. He died around 1769.

Dufays (Antoine), 1741

Ladroit was trustee around 1753. Rue Mazarine (1742-1755). Rue Saint-Honoré opposite the Oratoire (1755-1757). Rue Bourbon at the Ville-Neuve (now rue d'Aboukir, 1757-1760). Quai des Augustins (1760). Rue de la Harpe (1761).

Motet, at the Academie of Jouan (rue des Canettes, 1751). Near the rue de la Comédie-Française (rue de l'Ancienne Comédie, 1751). Rue de Seine (1760-1772).

---

Chris Slee, LongEdge Press, 2016

Feauveaux, rue du Jour (1755). Rue Saint-Martin (1760). Rue Michel-le-Comte (1769-1772).

Dalonneau de la Rate, master of arms to the Duke of Bourgogne, 1758

Thonnard, *juré* before 1755, trustee in 1757 and in 1761. He lived in 1760 near the Cross of Trahoir (this cross is situated on the corner of the rues de l'Abre-Sec and Saint-Honoré). Rue Christine (1761). Rue de Noyers (1776-1777). Rue de Viarmes (1777).

Chabot, rue de Bretonnerie (rue removed before the Revolution in order to increase the Place Saint Geneviève or the Panthéon) 1760.

Danet (Guillaume), author of a fencing treatise (1766-1767), squire, trustee, *Garde de l'Ordre*, master of arms of the squires of the Prince of Conti, director of the Royal School of Arms, Rue de Chantre (1760-1792).

Lasalle, received to the Mastery 1st March 1758. Rue Saint-Jean-de-Beauvais (rue Charretière, 1760). Rue de Boucheries-Saint-Germain (1769-1772).

Daniel (Pierre) trustee in 1754 and in 1755. Rue de la Monnaie (1760). Rue Saint-André-des-Arts (1769-1772).

Devocour, rue des Cordeliers (1760). Rue des Noyers (1772).

Le Perche, rue Mazarine, 1760

Guillaume, rue de Seine, 1760

Donnadieu, rue des Vieilles-Etuves (rue Sauvai, 1760-1769). Quai de l'Ecole (quai du Louvre, 1772-1789).

Rivière, rue des Fossés-Saint-Germain (rue de l'Ancienne Comédie, 1760). Rue de Vaugirard (1769-1772). Faubourg Saint-Honoré (1777).

La Boëssière (Texier de) received as master in 1759, master of arms of the pages of the Duke of Penthiévre. Rue de la Draperie (this street is situated opposite the Palais de Justice, 1769-1772). Rue Saint-Honoré, opposite the Oratoire (1806-1807).

O'Sullivan (Daniel) author of a fencing treatise, 1765. Rue du Jour-Saint-Eustache, in front of the gate, 1765. Passage du Saumon, 1769-1772.

Teillagorry brothers, nephews of Bertrand Teillagorry, in the stables of the Duke d'Orléans, 1769-1772. In 1789, one of the Teillagorry brothers lived on rue Neuve-des-Petits-Champs.

Dorcy (Guillaume), Île Saint-Louis, 1769-1772. He lived in 1789 in a house he owned at Préau the Market Saint-Germain (Place du Marché-Saint-Germain).

Prévost, senior (Louis) 1769-1790, master of arms of the pages of the King's Great and Little Stables; of the Queen's Stable; of the stable of Monsieur, of Madame, of the count of Provence, of the countess of Provence, of the countess of Artois, of the King's Chamber in 1786. Louis Prévost received as the price of his lesson to the page of the Madame's Household, 180 livres; the count of Provence, 100 livres; the countess of Artois, 180 livres. His fencing hall was located on the rue des Mauvais-Garçons (now the rue Grégoire-de-Tours), the first large gate on the left, entered by the rue de Buci. His own house was in the rue du Sépulchre (rue du Dragon), the first large gate on the left, entered by the rue Turanne (Boulevard Saint-Germain). Louis Prévost followed the court to Versailles.

Etienne the Elder, at the Royal Military School, 1769-1789

De Menissier, master of arms of the pages of the count of Clermont, was received to the mastery around 1764. Rue Sainte-Croix-de-la-Bretonnerie (1769-1772). Quai de la Tournelle (1789).

Lebrun, rue Montmartre, beside the Passage du Saumon around 1780

Pasquier or Paquier was deputy director of the Royal School of Arms. Cloître Saint-Thomas du Louvre (was located opposite the Place du Palais-Royal, 1769-1772). Rue du Sépulchre (rue du Dragon, 1789).

Ravet, rue aux Ours, 1769-1772.

Roch. Master of arms of the chamber of the count of Artois (he received 100 livres per year) 1774-1786. He was named master of the pages of the chamber of Monsieur in 1790. Roch followed the court to Versailles.

Prévost junior (François-Louis) had the remnant of the master of the pages of the Chamber, of the King's Great and Little Stables, as well as the pages of the stable of the count of Artois, 1786-1790. He was also master of arms of the Household of Condé. Prévost followed the court to Versailles.

Rousseau (Augustin-Bernard-Louis-Joseph), master of the exercise of arms to the Infants of France. Rousseau taught the exercises of war from 1774-1792 to the pages of the King's Great Stable; the handling of arms to the pages of the Little Stable; fencing to the pages of the Households of the Dukes of Angoulême and Berry. He followed the court. Rousseau was guillotined 13 July 1794.

Etienne the younger at the Royal Military School, 1789

Pauly, relative by marriage to Teillagorry. Little rue Saint-Louis (going from the rue de l'Echelle to the rue de Richelieu, 1789).

Leprince, rue de Richelieu, 1791

Pigeot, rue du Petit-Lion-Saint-Sauveur, 1791

Gomard. Rue du Bout-du-Monde (rue du Cadran) 1791. He had left the Bourbonnais Infantry regiment. Before opening a fencing hall, Gomard had been provost with La Boëssière. He adopted Antonin Possellier, called Gomard junior, who was in fencing one of the best theoreticians of the 19th century.

De la Boëssière junior, born in 1766, died in 1829, author of the fencing treatise (1818). 152 rue Saint-Honoré opposite the Oratoire and the Royal Armoury. 359 rue Saint-Honoré.

Famen (Philippe-Victor) born in 1754 and died here 6 August 1812. At the age of 19 years, he entered the house of La Boëssière senior where he became provost. We do not know if Fabien was part of the Company and if he had a fencing hall.

# List of Masters of the Royal School of Arms of the City of Paris who have made a Patriotic Offering of their Swords

31 December 1789

Teillagorry, director
Paquier, deputy director
Danet
Dorcy (Guillaume)
Donnadieu
Texier de la Boëssière
Prévost (Louis)
Prévost junior (François-Louis)
Le Valais
Lamare (Denis)
Desbuissons
La Boëssière, junior
Etienne the younger

Signatures from the 18th Century

Signatures from the 19th Century

Gervais
Desprès
De Menissier
Bouché

## Nineteenth Century

Renevier, 1809

Compoint, 1814

Coulon (Mathieu), 19 rue Cadet (1825-1827). 11 rue du Helder (1825-1830). 31 rue de Grammont (1831). 3 rue de Choiseul (1833-1838). 24 rue de Rivoli (1847).

Brémond, 10 rue du Faubourg-Poissonnière, 1814-1837

Gomard junior (aka Antonin Possellier) born in 1864. 18 rue de Chantre (1821-1828). 29 rue de Seine (1829-1834). 9 rue de Tournon (1835-1838). 33 rue Saint-André-des-Arts (1829-1841). Rue de la Houssaie (rue Taîtbout, 1842-1847).

Philippe the Elder, 1814. Rue Monsieur-le-Prince (1821-1829). Rue des Grès (rue Cujas, 1830).

Lamotte. 9 rue de Champs-Elysées (rue Boissy-d'Anglas, 1817). 9 Place du Palais-Royal (1820-1822). Rue Quincampoix (1823).

Charlemagne (aka François Vattier) born in 1779, died in 1857. 29 and 39 rue Traversière-Saint-Honoré (rue Molière, 1815-1828).

Bégo (Captain) 1816

Barbe (Olivier). 7bis rue de la Madeleine (1821-1824). 30 rue du Faubourg-du-Roule (rue du Faubourg-Saint-Honoré, 1825-1831).

Bertrand senior and junior. 31 rue Beauregard (1821). 367 rue Saint-Denis (1822).

Bertrand junior, born in 1796, died in 1876. 34 rue Saint-Thomas-du-Louvre (starting from the Place du Carrousel and ending at the Place du Palais-Royal, 1823-1827). 21 rue Poissonière (1828-1850). Bertrand has the second fencing hall on the rue and hôtel Corneille (1836-1838).

Bouquet. 7 rue Saint-Roch-Poissonière (part of the rue des Jeuneurs starting at the rue du Sentier and ending at the rue Poissonière, 1821). Rue Bergèr (1822).

De Saint-Marc. 37 rue Croix-des-Petits-Champs, 1821-1824

Deslauriers. 11 rue Rameau, 1821-1823

Gondemard, 9 rue des Grès (rue Cujas), 1821-1824

Lebrun junior. 21 rue Poissonière (1821-22). 29 Quai des Grands-Augustins (1823-1826). 72 rue Mazarine (his house was 33 rue Dauphine). 32 rue de Seine (1830). Rue des Marmousets (rue Chanoinesse, 1831-1837).

Dajon. 52 rue d'Anjou-Saint-Honoré (1825-1827). 16 rue de Cloître-Saint-Michel (This street was located near the rue de la Reine-Blanche, 1828-1829). 104 rue Saint-Jacques (1830-1836).

Lozis the Elder (Antoine), born in 1795, died in 1858. 9 rue des Grès (rue Cujas, 1825-1835).

Chardon. 31 rue d'Orléans-Saint-Marcel (rue Daubenton, 1826-1828). 5 Place de la Sorbonne (1829-1836). Rue du Cloître-Saint-Benoit (between the rue de la Sorbonne and rue Saint-Jacques, 1837-1838).

Colliquet. 21 or 24 rue des Filles-du-Calvaire (1827-1830). 2 or 3 rue Neuve-de-Bretagne (rue Commines, 1831-1834).

Blot (Jacques-Antoine). 33 rue des Petits-Carreaux (1829-1832). 6 rue Servandoni (1842).

Bouchez. 118 rue Saint-Jacques (1829-1835). 12 Place Saint-Michel (This place located opposite the rue des Grès (rue Cujas) has been absorbed by the boulevard Saint-Michel, 1836-1838).

Boulet. 39 rue Traversière-Saint-Honoré (rue Molière, 1829). 12 rue Favart (1830-1831). 255 rue Saint Martin (1832).

Buxe, 126 rue Saint-Jacques, 1829-1831

Graux, 40 rue Saint-Hyacinthe-Saint-Michel (rue Malebranche, 1829-1835)

Beau, 85 rue de la Harpe (boulevard Saint-Michel, 1832-1844)

Fillias, 32 rue de Miroménil (1832-1838). 11bis rue du Colisée (1839-1847).

Angot and Leverrier in 1834

Leverrier alone. 31 rue Bourbon-Villeneuve (today the rue d'Aboukir, the rue Bourbon-Villeneuve started at the rue Poissonière and ended at rue Saint-Denis) 1835-1839.

Grisier (Augustin), born in 1791, died in 1855. Rue de Tivoli (1832-1834). 4 rue du Faubourg-Montmartre (1834-1850).

Prévost (Pierre-Adolphe), born in Rouen in 1811, died in 1869. 33 rue des Boucheries-Saint-Germain (1833). 2 rue du Harlay-du-Palais (1834-1846). 12 rue de l'University (1847). 12 Passage Sainte-Marie (rue Saint-Simon, 1848-1850).

Daressy (Pierre), born in Agen in 1806, died at Paris in 1871. 20 rue J.-J. Rousseau (1834-1837). 113 rue Montmartre (1838-1844). 16 rue Notre-Dame-des-Victoires (1845-1848). 10 rue Faubourg-Montmartre (1848-1850).

Lozès (Bertrand), 5 rue Corneille, 1837

Lozès (?), rue des Francs-Bourgeois-Saint-Michel (this street was situated between the rue Monsieur-le-Prince and rue Soufflot, 1837)

Mille, 12 rue Favart, 1837

Mille and Rougé, 58 rue de la Harpe (boulevard Saint-Michel), 1837

Robert senior, 2 rue de l'Echaudé, 1837

Roger, rue du Dragon, 1837-1850

Roussel, 12 rue Favart, 1838-1843

Bénard, 1 rue de Rivoli, 1837-1850

Court. 219bis rue Saint-Honoré (1837). Rue Traversière-Saint-Honoré (rue Molière, 1838).

Alliac, 3 rue de Choiseul (1839). 4 rue Favart (1843-1847).

Raimondi (aka Réguzzoni) born in Lombardy in 1805, died in 1865. 27 rue Poissonière (1840). 39bis rue de la Fontaine-Molière (1846-1847). 10 rue Taitbout (1847-1850).

Bonnet, the Elder, born in 1801, died in 1873. 45bis rue de Richelieu (1848-1849). 41 rue de Richelieu (1840).

Pons, the uncle (Charles), born in 1795, died in 1883. 339 (new 223) rue Saint-Honoré.

Gatechair, senior

Renaudot

Franck

Marcelin

Dumesnil

Berrier

Robert, the Elder (Jean-Baptisce)

Cordelois, born in 1797, died in 1879. Was for a long time master of arms in Bordeaux before coming to Paris.

Pons, the nephew

Gatechair, junior (Hippolyte)

Ardohain, born in 1794, died in 1885.

# Principle Masters of Arms of Some Towns of France

Fontaine (Laurent), la Fére, 1572

Fontaine junior, Saint-Quentin, 1572

Souplet, Saint-Quentin, 1572

Ferron (Jacques) Brantôme's master of arms

Aymard (Sir) of Bordeaux

Plate, at Toulouse, 17th and 18th centuries

Besnard (Charles) at Rennes, 1653. Author of a treatise.

Labat, at Toulouse, 1696. Composed a celebrated book of fencing.

Martin, at Strasbourg, 1737. Author of a treatise.

Charpentier, at Lyon, 1742. Wrote a fencing treatise.

Gérard, Nancy

Siguion, Marseille, 1765

Simon, Lyon, 1766

Picard, Rouen, 1767

Faldoki, Lyon, 1767

Blondin, Agen, 1780

Labadie, Bordeaux, 1782

O'Sullivan junior, Angers, 1782

Moreau (Joseph), Nantes, 1782

## Nineteenth Century

Daressy (Jean), Agen
Prévost, Rouen
Moreau junior, Nances
Lafaugère (Louis- Justin), Lyon
Jean-Louis, Montpellier
Monsarrat senior, Toulouse
Vigeant (François), Rennes
Azaïs, Toulouse

# Fencing and Fencers (1556–1850)

## Sale by Mathieu Gossu to Jean Gossu

(Friday 8 May 1556)

In front of... etc... was present in person Matheiu Gossu, master swordsman[155] at Paris, living in the rue de la Vieille Pelleterie in the City, which by his good spirits and good will,[156] is recognised to have sold, ceded, quitted, transported, and forsaken immediately and forever...

... to Jehan Gossu his son, also master swordsman at Paris, rue de la Buscherie...

... one part of the garden and half of a farm situated in the village of Villons, near the manor house of the said place...

## Letter of Permission for Mathieu De Lor

(31 August 1570)

Charles, by the Grace of God King of France to our loved and faithful people of our Court of Parliament at Paris, the Provost of the said place or his lieutenant, greetings and affection. Be it known that we, having regard and consideration for the request which has been made to us in favour of Mathieu De Lor, Master of Arms of our town of Paris, have permitted and we permit him that he can and may lawfully[157] demonstrate and teach fencing in his house, of which he is the owner, situated on rue Saint-Jacques in the bishopric of Paris, with all

---

[155] *maistre joueur d'espee*
[156] *de son bon gré et de bonne volonté*
[157] *loisible*

types of weapons, to all persons who seem good to him and who want to take the exercise of the said weapons from the said De Lor.

Thus, we command and enjoin you, by these present letters with our present authorisation, license and permission, to suffer and to allow the said De Lor to use and to employ fully and peacefully without going nor coming nor suffering that he may go or come directly or indirectly to the contrary. Thus, if anything has been done or attempted to prejudice this permission, repair it and put it straightways back to a state of right. And this notwithstanding, the prohibitions made by you to the said De Lor and any ordinances, commands, prohibitions and letters to the contrary to these, together with the abolition of the abolishment of it,[158] we have in this regard and without prejudicing them in other things abolished and we abolish by the said present letters. For such is our pleasure.

Given at Paris, the last day of August year of grace 1570 and of our reign the tenth.

For the King,

Brulard

And sealed on a simple tail of yellow wax with the Great Seal.

## Warrant Accorded to Laurent Fontaine

(21 June 1572)
*Registered in the Chamber of the Council of the town of Saint-Quentin.*

If Laurent Fontaine, fencing master living at La Fère, wants to come to live in this town, it will be permitted for him to hold salle, like he has.

He cannot teach or hold an open salle during the divine service, on pain of 10 livres fine for both him and his host.

The same decision in regard to Henry Souplet and Fontain junior, fencing masters, living in this town, holding salle here.

## Receptions of Masters and Elections of *Jurés*

On 9 September 1586, on the report of the *Jurés*, fencers in deeds of arms of this town of Paris, Egard Musquin was received master, etc.

---

[158] *la dérogation de la dérogatoire d'icelle*

The same day Jean Petit the younger was similarly received as master. (They are both sons of masters of arms.)

Marcel Belly was received master by examination in 1587. The *Jurés* were: Jean Petit, Jean Langlois, Sébastien de Riquebourg and Marcel Duc.

---

On 23 April 1587, on the report of the *Jurés* in deeds of arms of this town of Paris, Gérard Papillon was made master in deeds of arms by masterwork and made the oath before Monsiegneur Déjardin, substitute for the King's Procurer General in the presence of the master P. Petit and C. Cochey *jurés* and other masters.

---

On 12 August 1587, Grandjean, Laloy, and Sébastien de Riquebourg were elected *Jurés*.

The masters who then obtained the greatest number of votes were Musquin, Alexandre Prévôt and Pierre Vallet.

---

On 2 December 1587, Jean Langlois, son of Jean Langlois, was received master.

---

30 May 1588
*Jurés* elected

| | |
|---|---|
| Pierre Chaudière | 8 votes |
| Alexandre Prévôt | 8 votes |

After them Pierre Vallet had the greatest number of votes.

---

22 August 1589
*Jurés* elected

| | |
|---|---|
| Pierre Charenny | 10 votes |
| Jean Lecoq | 8 votes |

7 July 1590
   *Jurés* elected

| Claude Charpentier | 10 votes |
| Jean Langlois | |
| Nicolas Dubuisson | |

30 September 1594
   *Jurés* elected
Alexandre Prévôt, replacing Marcel Dubuisson

12 August 1602
   *Jurés* elected

| Pierre Vallet | 10 votes |
| Nicolas Dubuisson | 10 votes |

27 January 1604
Jacques Bourdon was elected *Juré* replacing Pierre Vallet

# Cavalcabo

In the 15th century, a patrician family from Cremona carried the name Cavalcabo.

In 1588, Zacharia Cavalcabo reprinted in Bologna, at the house of Gino Rossi, the fencing treatise that Viggiani dal Mantone of Bologna had published in 1575.

In 1609, a French gentleman, lord Villamont, published a book whose title is:

> Treatise or Instruction for the use of arms, from the excellent fencer Hyéronime Cavalcabo, Bolognese, with an ad-

dress for using the sword alone made by the late Patenostrier of Rome.[159]

Translated from Italian into French by the lord Villamont, Knight of the Order of Jerusalem and gentleman of the King's Chamber.

At Rouen, at the house of Claude Le Villain, the King's bookseller and bookbinder, living on rue du Bec, at the Good Reputation.

Dedicated to the Marshall, Count of Brissac.

Would not Hiéronyme Cavalcabo be the master of arms to Louis XIII and the father of César Cavalcabo?

# Jacques Ferron

Brantôme's master of arms was named Jacques Ferron. He was born at Asté, a city situated near Bagnères-de-Bigorre.

Jacques Ferron was killed at Sainte-Bazeille in the month of April 1586 during the siege of this small village by the Duke of Mayenne.

---

[159] Hieronymus Calvacabo of Bologna and Patenostrier of Rome, *Treatise or Instruction for Fencing*, trans. Rob Runacres, Lulu.com (2015), ISBN 978-1-326-16469-0

# Essay on the Marvels of Nature

*by Rene François,*
*Preacher to the King*
*Rouen, 1622*

Pastor Étienne Binnet, King's Preacher, published in 1622 (under the pseudonym Réné François) a type of encyclopaedia in one volume, having for its title *Essay des merveilles de nature* [Essay on the Marvels of Nature]. This book obtained success: we know of in it up to thirteen editions. One chapter of this book, dedicated to *The Use of Arms*, furnishes us with very curious information about the terms in use in the fencing halls in the time of Louis XIII.

It is in this work that we find for the first time the word *fleuret*[160] written as in our times.

Several authors of the 16th century – Étienne Pasquier in his *Des Recherches de la France* [Some Research about France, 1596], Montaigne in his *Essays* – wrote *floret*.

"A rude fencer, foil in hand" (Montaigne)

## The Use of Arms

1.

One calls the foil [*la fleuret*], or brette, a rebated sword without a point. The button [*le bouton*] is the end of the sword drawn back and collected in a knot. The end [*le bout*] of the foil is a ball or padded leather that one puts on the end so that in giving[161] one does not kill. Also, one says to a boy, "put an end on the foil."

2.

The guard [*la garde*] is that which is on the handle to cover the hand. The strong [*le fort*] is about a foot in length from the guard. The remainder up to the tip is called the weak [*le foible*] of the sword.

---

[160]ie: foil
[161]The French do not 'make strikes', they *give* them and *receive* them

3.

When one is presented in the salle, we ask "monsieur, do you want to do?" or "do you want to make an assault?", that is to say, "do you want to fence?".

Then, taking up and uncrossing weapons, or even with honour kissing them, we say: "messieurs, protect your eyes," that is to say, we forbid each other to strike to the face.

If a mishap occurs, that the strike escapes and that one strikes the face,[162] immediately we all put weapons down and go gather around him who received and pray him excuse the accident.

4.

The Fencing Master almost never fights but there is a provost, that is to say, a lieutenant or sub-master who fights and who supports all combat.

The Master sees, instructs, gives the stop [*holà*] when the blood is heated, marks the faults and judges the strikes.

5.

The good strikes are called unimpeded thrusts[163] when the foil marks the assured strike and gives straight on and in full. If it is only half, perhaps in passing, they say it misses.

6.

One should be in measure for giving and receiving a strike, that is to say, one should fix the right foot firmly in front and in a posture confident but nimble.[164]

To be out of measure is when one is either too advanced in danger of falling or to lean in and grab the enemy, or too withdrawn, or the foot in the air and the body wavering, or too fixed.

---

[162] *qu'on le porte au visage*
[163] *bottes franches*
[164] *isnelle*

### 7.

One is said to be in school, that is to say, to well adjust his body and carry it straight as he ought as if one said "protect the button." For to adjust and to be in school, one should give straight in the button.

If one does not do it, we say that one is not in school, that is to say that one has forgotten, or even that one has not yet learned the terms and the strikes of the school. One says also to adjust the strike or not to adjust.[165]

### 8.

One should always have a wary eye on the enemy, above all, on his eyes, for often he darts his glance to where he will direct[166] the point of his sword. Thus, one can put oneself on defence.

When one raises the right foot in order to advance, one calls that the tempo. From there, to take the tempo is about advancing. To gain the tempo is to anticipate your man and while he arranges himself to take his tempo you anticipate it. Thus, to lose one's tempo is when one knows not how to manage this advancing of the feet.

### 9.

One says to carry a thrust, to receive it, to parry, to give, to drive down his man, to retire the foot behind, to do a slip backwards, to loose[167] the foot, to give a leap.

After the strike, one should soon put oneself again in measure, that is to say, the right foot in front planted very firmly and the body settled. Otherwise, one easily staggers.

### 10.

There are several feints, the high, the straight, the low, around the dagger, to the eyes.

The simple-minded amuse themselves to make parries and some feints in the air and play the fool,[168] but one should always take the feint for the strike, for often one strikes without a feint, and to do well the strike should follow immediately the feint.

---

[165] *on dit aussi ajuster le coup, ou non ajuster*
[166] the word used is *porter* (to carry) which is used in the same way as in tennis
[167] *lascher*
[168] *faire la beste*

Also, the foot and the hand should also fly all in one tempo.

Never should one withdraw the arm and the foot in order to give better and with the greater force. It is a popular error.

Never should one retreat but always advance and push. For in retiring in order to give, the enemy sees the strike come and while you retire, he anticipates you and gives to you.

### 11.

Opening oneself and giving oneself in person is when either in order to draw out your enemy and deceive him or by carelessness you separate the weapons and show all of your stomach and all your person, making it easy for your enemy to pierce you fully through.[169] To close up, on the contrary, is to join his weapons and to almost cover his person with the foil and sidesword[170] or dagger.

### 12.

The riposte is named when one gives and one receives almost in the same tempo. Also, one says this "at the prompt riposte" for he answers you and returns to you identically[171] the strike that you have given him.

Those who have weapons well in hand do not fear the riposte, inasmuch as the strong of their sword shields them.

### 13.

He who knows well how to handle the sword has hardly anything to do with the dagger for parrying the strikes. For from the strong he takes the weak, that is to say, he receives the point of his enemy's sword on the strong of his own and makes it pass by in the air and beats it away or at least avoids the strike.

One of the great secrets is to know well how to best use the strong of one's sword. It is an invention of a brave master of swordplay.

---

[169] *faisant beau jeu a vostre ennemy pour vous percer*
[170] *l'espee blanche*, like *l'arme blanche* or sidearm
[171] *tout aussi tout*

14.

One says "pass" when one opens himself too much or, not being on his guard, the other gives him a strike full, straight and as if he wanted to pass him through the stomach and, after having given him the crosswise strike,[172] he wants to overturn him onto the tiles. Yet, if he to whom one carries this strike turns himself sideways, throwing again the right foot behind, the strike passes by in the air and moreover carries the thrust directly to the heart of him who wanted to give and that is called the fourth,[173] that is to say, in avoiding the strike of him who wants to pass by us when we pass the sword across the body, we have turned away a little sidestep and pierce him.

15.

We do not use at this time cuts, *estramaçons* and similar strikes. All pass now in thrusts and giving the point rather than the edge of the sword. For they [ie: cutting strikes] are the knocks and true strikes of the Swiss and Germans, (and) that these backhand strikes and [forehand] strikes draw back with force the arm in order to cleave a shoulder or cut the thighs clean through, etc.

---

[172] *le coup à travers*
[173] *quarter*

# A Fencing Competition at Toulouse

Under the reign of Louis XIII, the masters of arms of Toulouse, with the aim of inspiring emulation among their students, resolved to meet these latter in an annual conference and to determine the prize to two victors of this tourney.

A gilded silver[174] sword was the recompense for the first. The second received a silver sword. A little later, the chief magistrates[175] and the body of the city supported the expense of these prizes in the town of Toulouse, with which the weapons were engraved on the sword blades.

They agreed further, to those who merited them, free entry to the spectacle and the right to be presented with the sword at the town hall.

He should be of a noble or honourable family in order to take part in this competition which took place at same moment as that of the *Jeux Floraux*.[176]

M. de Montandier, lawyer and chief magistrate under Louis XIV, revived this custom which had begun to fall into disuse.

In 1754, the eldest master of arms of Toulouse was Plate, whose father, grandfather and great-grandfather had taught fencing.

The great-grandfather had even been one of the promoters of the establishment of the prize.

# The Master of Arms by Bonnart

An engraving by Bonnart,[177] who lived under Louis XIV, shows a master of arms in the costume of the period. At the bottom of the engraving is the following quatrain:

> Rather than one knowing how without shame
> The least touches to endure,
> This master, in stuffing himself,
> Finds his honour and his score.

---

[174] *vermeil*

[175] *les capitouls* – the twelve chief magistrates of the city

[176] A poetry and minstrelsy festival and competition revived in Toulouse in 1324 and lasting until 1790. It was re-established in 1806 and continues to the present day

[177] This images is not reproduced in the original book

## Pierre Daniel

Pierre Daniel, before being master of arms, fought a duel and killed his adversary.

Not able to obtain letters of remission, he took refuge in Orléans and waited there until a new bishop would find in his favour [by] the custom of his episcopal right.

Until the Revolution, the bishops of Orléans possessed the authority which they exercised the day of their consecration, at the moment of their solemn entry into the town.

Under the Restoration, Monseigneur de Varicourt succeeded, at his installation, in reviving this authority.

This was for the last time.

## Bertrand Teillagorry

### Declaration of Cens

(28 August 1750)

Today the undersigned appeared before the councillors of the King notaries in the Châtelet of Paris.

Eléonore Delamant, wife not of common goods[178] of Sir Bertrand Teillagorry, master in deeds of arms at Paris, and previously widow of Sir Nicolas Deneux, living at Paris, rue Neuve-des-Petits Champs, parish of Saint-Eustace, declared and recognised to be holder[179] and owner of a house situated at Paris, rue Saint-Honore, which she takes in order to teach at the City of Constantinople, now occupied by Sir Lasalle, haberdasher.

## Dorcy

1770

Dorcy, master of arms of the King's Academies, makes a declaration in the region of Paris, for a house which he possesses at Préau from the Saint Germain Market.

---

[178] *épouse non commune de biens*. Presumably meaning a wife with property in her own right.
[179] *detemptrice*. From *détenteur*, legitimate possessor?

## Lefebvre, His Provost Warrant Annulled

From 1750 to 1753, three complaints had been written in the Community's register against a provost of Daniel named Pierre-Antoine Lefebvre.

The first complaint holds that he had threatened master Feauveaux even in his own salle. The second that he had twice forced his master, Pierre Daniel, to take his sword in hand on the Place du Louvre near the Luxembourg.

Finally, he had insulted Bertrand Teillagorry as well as several other masters.

In a judgement in the form of advice given 9 February 1753 by the King's Procurer at the Châtelet, the Lieutenant General of Police, on the 23rd of the same month, broke Lefebvre's warrant[180] and declared him incapable of being master in deeds of arms.

Despite this judgement Lefebvre persisted and the same year presented himself to the mastery, supported by the good will of his master Daniel who was then Trustee, and in this capacity had even received in advance the sum of 789 livres reception dues owed to the Community.

The masters of arms refused to proceed with his examination.

Vainly Lefebvre pleaded against the Company. The trial, which lasted some time, ended with an injunction of the Court of Parliament declaring Lefebvre forfeited all rights to the mastery.

## Guillaume Danet

Guillaume Danet, the famous author of the treatise *L'Art des Armes* [The Art of Arms, 1766], was several times Trustee and *Garde de l'Ordre* of the Company.

Since the appearance of the first volume of his work (1766), Danet had much to complain of [about] his fellows. Whether from habit or jealousy,[181] the majority did not want to recognise the justness of the innovations brought by Danet to the art of fencing.

La Boëssière himself lent his pen[182] to the little war made against Danet, and directed in the name of the Company the critique of his treatise.

---

[180] *brevet*
[181] *Par esprit de routine ou par jalousie*
[182] *préta le concours sa plume*

But in the second volume which appeared the year following, Danet victoriously refuted the arguments of his adversaries. Posterity sees him as correct.[183]

Danet was master of arms to the pages of the Prince of Conti. In 1789, he received 120 livres per year as the price of his lessons.

Danet was the first director of the Royal School of Arms of the city of Paris.

## La Boëssière, senior

Texier de La Boëssière was born 23 July 1723 at Marans, a little village situated near La Rochelle.

La Boëssière's parents had destined him from his youth to the ecclesiastical vocation.[184] He preferred to be master of arms.

Upon his reception to the mastery, which took place in 1759, he was tested by the last three masters received into the Community: Donnadieu, Delasalle and Devocour.

In 1766, when Danet published his first volume on fencing, the Company charged La Boëssière with directing the critique of it. It appeared under the title *Observations sur le traité de l'Art des armes, pour servir de défense à la vérité des principes enseignés par les maîtres d'armes de Paris, par M\*\*, maître d'armes des Académies du Roi, au nom de la Compagnie, 1766* [Observations on the Treatise of the Art of Arms, in order to serve the defence of the truth of the principles taught by the Masters of Arms of Paris, by M \*\*, the master of arms of the King's Academies in the name of the Company, 1766].

This critique was an error that the master who shaped so many brilliant students must have regretted more than once.

La Boëssière had a taste for *belles-lettres*. He wrote several pieces of theatre, among them a comedy *Crispin valet d'auteur* [Crispin, Valet of the Author], an opera *La Coquette à la campagne* [The Coquette of the Country]. He also made several [books of] poetry.

If renown was not attached to his name as poet and dramatic author, he had at least as master of arms the glory of having taught the famous knight of Saint George.

To this celebrated name, we add those of Gomard senior, Cavin, Saint-Laurent, la Madeleine, Pomart and La Boëssière junior, the author of a fencing treatise.

---

[183] *la postérité lui donna raison*
[184] *l'état ecclésiastique*

Texier La Boëssière died at Paris 1 May 1807 at the age of 84 years. Three months before, he still gave fencing lessons.

It seems interesting to us to give the preface of his poem on the death of a prince of Brunswick-Lunebourg.

This prince perished in 1785, victim of his devotion in carrying himself to the help of two unfortunates who drowned.

We follow this preface with the letter that La Boëssière wrote, in the year 12, to the government commissioner attached to the Théatre-Français and the response of the commissioner to this letter.

Its topic is stanzas composed by La Boëssière, then at the age of 80 years.

## The Noble Death Of Prince Léopold of Brunswick

Elegiac Poem by
M. Texier de la Boëssière

Master of Arms of the King's Academies and of the Pages of His Highness, Most Serene Monseigneur, the Duke of Penthièvre

> *He who descends into the tomb through his humanity*
> *Is a hero who rises to immortality*

At Paris
At the house of the Author
Bailly, bookseller, rue Saint-Honoré, opposite *la Barrière des Sergents*
And the Novelty Merchants[185]
MDCCLXXXVI

## Preface

Sensibility, rather than poetical talent, schooled me and made me celebrate the heroic devotion of Prince Léopold of Brunswick. My piece finished, I wanted to judge its effects. I read it to three people separately.

At the end of the recounting of the event or death of the heroes, all three answered equally with tears. Although I had the applause of nature, I lacked the opinion of art.

---

[185] *les Marchands des Nouveautés*

I had the temerity to send the work to the *Académie Française* in order to participate in the competition that a great Prince, sensitive and generous, had announced.

The severe *Académie*, who judged that it should be acceptable, declared itself a little satisfied and gave it the prize in 1787.

From this moment, the Zoïles of the Clubs and Cafes began to brighten at the expense of poor competitors.

These gentlemen knew that I was among their number but they did not know my work. I had not the least part in their sarcasm, their cautious causticity dropping always indirectly.

I have not the foolish vanity of raising myself to Parnassus but I want to be judged such that I am. This reason appears to me sufficient in order for me to decide to print [it].

Deciding not to enter the competition again, I opened myself to a man famous for his literary knowledge. He counselled me to retouch my piece in several places and to send it to a second competition. I profited, losing no time, as much as I could, from the first review[186] but no aspiration could dissuade me from publishing my homage to the ashes of Léopold, and to the Persons that I celebrate, other powerful reasons still engaging me to take this course.

I am of an age where the man who reasons according to the balance of probabilities sees himself uncertain of surviving the next year.

I professed for thirty years an art in which I have earned, without charlatanry, the public confidence.

Since that time, always occupied, I have had few moments to give to literature, and though I have received from nature some germs of talent, having so little cultivated them, I cannot claim today the perfection required by the *Académie*.

Moreover, a Poet accustomed to gather the laurels, a famous Academician, a competition judge addressed the proposed subject, but in assuring with an honest decency that does not extend to thwart the competitor's interests.

He read his product to the *Académie* where it obtained a popular and deserved vote.[187]

Siding always with the principle of disinterest, of which he has always given proofs, he carried his work to Versailles and had it passed to the Courts of Germany.

After this, if I were to return to this career, would I not look like a pygmy who wants to raise himself to the height of a large man? I

---

[186] *premier avis*
[187] *un suffrage général et mérité*

will not give myself to this ridicule and, fearing the temptation, I will print it.

If I have the misfortune to be badly received[188] by the public, it will be a lesson which will prevent me from irritating them a second time, curing me of the urge that I have to bring into the light a number of works, the timid infants of my leisure.

I will throw them ruthlessly on the fire. I will break my sad lyre. Then, restraining me in my state, I will console myself with pride and will say "Racine made *Phèdre* but I made *Saint-George*."

---

Citizen,

The stanzas that I have the honour to address to you were presented handwritten to the First Consul by the Consul Cambacérès.[189] They were so well-received that it engaged me to print them. I addressed the first copies to the First Consul. On the same day, citizen Maret, Councillor of State and General Secretary of the Government, wrote to me and announced to me the satisfaction of the First Consul. He indicated to me at the same time the means of passing them to the chiefs of the officer corps[190] of the English army, which I have done through the minister of war.

Consul Lebrun to whom I also sent some copies thanked me by a letter in his hand. In these circumstances, I have a favour to ask of you, citizen commissioner. Can one not have it recited between two plays at the Theatre of the Republic and on a day you judge appropriate? If you don't want to take that on yourself, speak of it, I pray you, with the minister of the interior and with the prefect of the palace if it concerns you. I don't believe that they will oppose themselves to it. We are in a moment where one cannot animate too greatly the national spirit against a minister so perfidious as that of England. It would give these stanzas more publicity and would put me in the position of sending a greater number of copies to the armies, not having made a great enough number to give away.

With regard to the artists of the Theatre Français, I have friends among them and they have too much patriotism [for me] to believe that they [would] refuse it.

---

[188] *mal accueilli*
[189] Jean-Jacques-Régis de Cambacérès, 1st Duke of Parma (later 1st Duke of Cambacérès)
[190] *états-majors*

It remains for me, citizen, to ask one more favour of you. This is of letting me to know your decision, since I do not want to publish any of the copies I have in hand before knowing that which you have decided.

I will be with recognition and respect your devoted servant,

La Boëssière

Master of Arms, 45 rue Honoré, opposite the Oratory

The 12 Vendémiaire, Year 12[191]

## The Cry of Vengeance on the Breaking of the Peace and the Infamy of the English Ministers

Presented to the First Consul

Stanzas dedicated to the French Army
By Citizen La Boëssière

Author of the Ode to Peace after the Ratification of the Treaty of Amiens, beginning thus:

> Achieved by Mars divine peace
> Fixes happiness on earth,
> etc

To citizen La Boëssière,
Master of Arms, 45 rue Honoré, opposite the Oratory:
Paris, 6 October 1803, Year 12

Citizen,

I received the stanzas that you composed against the infamy of the English ministers and that did the honour of addressing me. I hasten to thank you for them and of adding my particular voice to the votes, most brilliant but not sincere, that you have obtained from the chief magistrates of the Republic. You desire that in order to give more publicity to these stanzas that they be recited in the Theatre Français. It would be agreeable to me to be able to gratify this circumstance, but

---

[191] 5 October 1803

an injunction of the government several times renewed by the police forbids artists singing anything, reciting anything that may be foreign to their roles and the rule particular to the comedy[192] prescribes not performing even in the roles of the ancient plays any type of changes without them having been submitted to the censure of the Prefect of the Palace.

According to these very formal ordinances[193] you ascertain, citizen, the rigorous obligation where I find myself only allowed to decide for the Theatre Français that which is found in the plays approved by the government.

Please therefore receive my excuses on the impossibility in which I find myself of doing that which you wish and accept with my regrets the salute of my highest consideration.

## The Knight Saint-George

The life of the Knight Saint-George was made in order to tempt biographers: indeed, it has been described several times.

We are above all indebted to La Boëssière junior for leaving us, in his fencing treatise, very precious information about his father's student.

Saint-George was born at Gaudeloupe on 25 December 1745. He was a mulatto.

The father, M. de Boulgne, (who became a *fermier général*[194]) brought him to Paris at the age of 10 years and gave him a brilliant education.

Saint-George was 13 years old when he was boarded in the house of La Boëssière senior. He remained here six years. Mornings were used in his education. He passed the rest of the day in the training hall.

He learned with the greatest ease all that his masters taught him.

His progress in fencing was no less rapid.

At 15 years old, says La Boëssière, he beat the strongest fencers. At 17 years, he had acquired the greatest speed. In time, he joined to prompt execution an understanding which succeeded in making him incomparable.

Saint-George preserved this speed until he was forty years old. At this age, he tore the Achilles tendon of his left foot. This accident

---

[192] *Comédie Française?*
[193] *ordonnances aussi formelles*
[194] combination tax and lease collector for the crown

happened while dancing at a ball.

Saint-George reached the height of five foot six inches (1.782m). He was very well-made and was gifted with prodigious bodily strength.

A good horseman, elegant dancer, tireless swimmer, all the exercises of the body were familiar to him. He excelled in them all.

He won, in England, a bet of five hundred pounds on the Prince of Wales by clearing a jump over the large ditches[195] of the Richmond castle.

A remarkable violinist, he left some concertos and above all a famous minuet which carried his name.

Nevertheless, we must add that he tried composing several comic operas but he did not succeed here.

At the end of the year 1775, the Opera being on the point of being put under regulation,[196] several companies presented themselves. Saint-George, who was at the head of one of them, was on the verge of obtaining management of the theatre.

But Sophie Arnould, Guimard, Rosalie, etc, informed of this fact, immediately addressed a petition to the Queen, representing to her that their honour and the delicacy of their consciences would not permit them being under the command of a mulatto.

The incident was very embarrassing. After a great number of negotiations, the king cut through the difficulty by arranging manage the Opera on his own account.

Saint-George entered the musketeers, was captain of the guards of the Duke of Chartres, master of the hounds and superintendent of music of the Duke of Orléans.

He was also page to Mme de Montesson.

During the Revolution, Saint-George raised a regiment of light cavalry which he led with the army of the north.

On 27 September 1792, he sent a letter to the National Assembly in order to announce the taking of Saint-Amand and the lifting of the siege of Maulde.

Some time after, he was arrested on suspicion and only achieved his salvation on 9 Thermidor.[197]

Saint-George developed, around the age of fifty-four years, an ulcer which he neglected to have treated. Gangrene ensued and occasioned his death, occurring at Paris on 12 June 1799.

---

[195] moat?
[196] into receivership?
[197] 27 July presumably 1793

Saint-George's Signature

We give a facsimile of Saint-George's signature in the following piece. As superintendent of music to the Duke of Orléans, he gave his approval to the amounts carried on this account.

## Account of Musicians Used in Spectacles for the Service of Monseigneur

| | | |
|---|---|---|
| Lescuyer | 4 times | 96 livres |
| Lefebvre | 3 – | 36 – |
| Pradere | 4 – | 48 – |
| Rousseau, Elder | 3 – | 36 – |
| Rousseau, junior | 3 – | 36 – |
| Menel | 3 – | 36 – |
| Piquot | 4 – | 48 – |
| Chelard | 3 – | 36 – |
| Lidski. | 2 – | 30 – |
| Danner, solo | 4 – | 60 – |
| Giuliano, solo | 3 – | 48 – |
| Fiorillo, solo | 4 – | 60 – |
| Blondeau | 3 – | 36 – |
| Total.... | | 606 livres |

Mr President

Saint-George, whose patriotism is well-known since the Revolution and according to the conduct that he showed at Lille in Flanders where he resided two years and where he commanded a company of national guard which he left in order to serve in the capacity of aide-de-camp voluntarily to Messers Duhon and Miaizinscky who conjointly with every citizen responded to his patriotism, has accepted the command of the Hussars of the Midi, desiring to continue and to immortalise himself by his valour and his enthusiasm for liberty. Only able to prove his zeal and assure success with his sleek body and approved by the different sections whose civil spirit[198] he cherishes, he hopes to be seconded by them in wanting to approve or disapprove the enlistments that he will have the honour of addressing to them successively.

He has the honour to be, Mr President, your very humble and very obedient servant,

Saint-George

---

*Letters similar to that above were probably sent to all the presidents of the sections of Paris. The letter that we possess is only signed by Saint-George.*

## Augustin Rousseau

Augustin-Bernard-Louis-Joseph Rousseau was born at Versailles around 1748.

Coming from a family of illustrious masters of arms, he became himself the fencing teacher to the Infants of France.

Arrested on 10 August 1792, incarcerated on the 18th of the same month at the abbey, Rousseau was transferred to another prison before the massacres of 2 September.

But, if he escaped the assassins led by ex-warden Maillard, his punishment was only delayed.

Included in a contingent[199] of twenty-eight persons brought on 23 Messidor of the year 2 (13 July 1794) before the revolutionary tribunal sitting in the Chamber of Liberty, he was like his co-accused condemned to death and executed the same day.

The act of accusation quantified him "a conspirator having been arrested 10 August at the Château des Tuileries, dressed in the dress of the national uniform wearing a rallying button."

---

[198] *civisme*
[199] *fournée*

| DÉPARTEMENT DE POLICE | MUNICIPALITÉ DE PARIS. |

*[handwritten document]*

N°. 87. Le Concierge de l'Abbaye recevra de MM. Rousseau Préposé de la Police Municipale et P. le Appariteur de Versailles Le S. Rousseau Maître d'Armes des Enfants de France et le gardera jusqu'à nouvel ordre. Les Administrateurs de Police, Membres de la Commission de Surveillance.

A la Mairie le 8. 9bre 1792. l'an 1er de la Liberté.

*Rossignol*
*Buel*  *Duffort*
*Duchesne*

Department of Police, Municipality of Paris

After the pronouncement of the sentence of death, one of the judges cried, "Parry that, Rousseau!"

The Monitor[200] of 25 Messidor carried, "Rousseau ... Master of exercise and arms of the Capet Infants."

Mme Campan was Augustin Rousseau's sister-in-law.

Amédée, the youngest of the sons of the unfortunate Rousseau, was born at Versailles around 1790.

Under the name of Amédée de Beauplan, he published a great amount of sheet music. Several of his romances had great success.

Amédée Rousseau, who died at Paris in 1853, had taken the name of Beauplan from land that his mother owned near Chévreuse.

---

## Letter addressed to Citizen Antoine, the Pavillion before Orléans, 21 rue de Union, at Versailles.

24 Messidor, 11pm[201]

You have been much deceived, my poor dear and adored Julie, at the hopes which you have been given. Here I am at the last step of the persecutions exercised against me.

I await with the calm of innocence my act of accusation which must be signified to me in the night. I will carry to the tribunal the courage which purity of conscience inspires.

I will use all my means in order to convince the honest judges[202] that I have always been the friend of my country, and if the appearances often deceptive make me submit to a judgement that I have the certainty of not having merited, I will only make of it that it is in a time of revolution that the innocent may be struck.

My only regret, my dear and adored Julie, is of being separated from you, from my children, from our love.

I will pass the night thinking of you, and if I succumb, I will be happy for you all.

I recommend keeping your courage. It is the only mark of attachment that you can give to my memory.

I ask that your friend is never separated from you; I rely on it. I engage my daughters to preserve for you at all times the tenderness and the respect which they owe to your virtues.

---

[200] The official newspaper of the Revolutionary period
[201] 12 July 1794
[202] *juges intègres*

Rousseau's Signature

I ask them as well as you to excuse the modest petulance I had regarding them and you. My heart is well enough known to you in order [for you] to believe they are not blameable.

I hope that Auguste will console you with the best conduct and that he will replace me in searching to procure for you a type of happiness.

I hope for Amédée's qualities. He will give you satisfaction.

It is 10pm and I receive my act of accusation. It is founded on my rallying cry buttons and on that I had been arrested at the château on 10 August.

I will not have difficulty defending myself against this falsehood and the justice of the tribunal gives me all place to hope.

Farewell, my beautiful. Have courage, I beg of you. Receive the assurance of the attachment which will never end with me.

I kiss tenderly my children, my aunt and your love which I hope will remain mine.

They removed Josephine's medallion and the two rings from me.

I kiss you a thousand times. Tomorrow at midday my fate will be decided.

---

# Three Masters of Arms become Marshals of France

We read in the memoires of the Baron of Vitrolles that three Marshals of France had masters in their youth.

Augereau gave fencing lessons at Locle, a small Swiss village, then at Naples which he left in order to come to take up service in France.

Lefebvre had been master of arms in the French Guards.

Regarding Bernadotte, the future king of Sweden had been at the start of his military career a provost in the regiment of Royal Marines.

## Bouting in the Gardens of the Palais-Royale

Around the end of the reign of Louis XVI, there existed a stage[203] in the garden of the Palais-Royal. Assaults of arms were frequently given there and pitted masters against amateurs. During these bouts, which began at 5am, pieces of music were played. The price of entry was fixed at twenty-four sols.

## Charlemagne

Charlemagne (François-Charlemagne Vattier) was born at Falaise on 28 January 1779. He was captain of the equipment train of the Guard in 1814. The following year, he left military service and founded a training hall which became one of the most renown de Paris. Charlemagne retired in 1841 but he continued to give lessons in arms to the princes of Orléans.

Charlemagne died in November 1857 at Mainville (Seine-et-Oise).

Around 1830, a provost of Charlemagne made an assault with a student, the foil of this latter broke and the broken blade[204] penetrated into the upper arm, near the armpit, seriously injuring the provost.

So as to avoid the recurrence of accidents of this type, Charlemagne added to all the jackets the skin which now covers the right arm, from the shoulder to the middle of the arm.

## Jean Daressy

Jean-Anselme Daressy, son of an employee to the sub-delegate of the bishop of Agen,[205] was born in this town, rue Saint-Hilaire, on 14 April 1770.

Near his family home,[206] a master of arms named Blondin held an "Academy," as it was called.

---

[203] *cirque*
[204] *tronçon*
[205] a junior administrative official looking after a portion of the bishopric
[206] *la maison paternelle*

An imperfectly frosted window pane allowed the curious to see the interior of this salle. Thus, the young Daressy, returning home from school and knowing this peculiarity, benefited from watching the fencers practice.

Blodin, surprised by this diligence, questioned the child who explained his desire to learn to fence.

Blondin presented to Daressy senior the son's taste for arms and proposed to teach him the principles of his art.

The proposal[207] was well-received and in a few years Jean Daressy became a very good and above all a very elegant fencer.

A soldier from the end of the year 1793, thus his service record:[208]

**Daressy (Jean-Anselme)**
Entered 12th Regiment of Hussars – 7 December 1793
Corporal,[209] 7 December 1793
Sergeant, 30 January 1794
First Sergeant, 20 August 1794
Adjutant, 23 November 1795
Under-Lieutenant, 9 November 1796
Resigned, 27 April 1800

**Campaigns**
Army of the West: 1795-1796-1797-1798-1799
Army of Italy: 1799-1800

After having resigned his commission,[210] Jean Daressy returned to Agen where he obtained employment in the government.

As this post only took up part of his time, he benefited in his leisure in indulging[211] his passion for fencing.

He even installed in his house, rue du Marchéau-Blé, a training hall which became a meeting place for the amateurs of the town and for masters passing through Agen.

Jean Daressy also gave lessons and trained some distinguished fencers among whom we must cite first of all Justin Lafaugère, then Messers. Dutroil, Dufaure, de Campels, Martinelli, Gouget, Debédat, Roux-Lassalle, Rouilles, Desparbès, Campistron, etc.

---

[207] *demande*
[208] *voici le relevé de ses états de service*
[209] The text has *Brigadier*
[210] *avoir donné sa démission d'officier*
[211] *en se livrant*

His two sons, Pierre and Adolphe Daressy, were equally his students.

Jean Daressy died at Agen on 20 December 1821.

## La Boëssière, junior

La Boëssière, son of Saint George's master of arms, published a fencing treatise in 1818.[212] The author, desiring to present his work to the Minister of the Interior, wrote him the following letter.

> To his Excellency, My Lord the Minister of the Interior and Secretary of State
>
> My lord,
>
> I would like to present to Your Excellency a work which I have composed on my art and that I presented recently to His Majesty and to Yourself.
>
> I beseech Your Excellency to summon me to him in whichever of his precious moments that he would like to accord me in order that I could offer him my work.
>
> I have the honour of being with profound respect,
>
> My lord,
>
> Your very humble and very obedient servant,
>
> La Boëssière
> Master of Arms at the former King's Academies and Royal Household, 152 rue Saint-Honoré

La Boëssière omitted to add (conveniently forgot[213]) that from 1806 to 1814 he had been fencing teacher to the Pages of the Emperor.

---

[212] *Traité de l'art des armes* [Treatise on the Art of Arms]
[213] *oubli volontaire*

# Lafaugère

Louis-Justin Lafaugère was born at Agen on 8 August 1782. In the fencing treatise which he published in 1820, he gave some information on his life that we reproduce succinctly, fixing with some dates the facts recounted by him.

We complete his biography and follow it with some anecdotes that we have from people worthy of credence.[214]

1800

Lafaugère begins the study of fencing at the house of Jean Daressy.

1802

He enters the 25th Light Cavalry regiment[215] garrisoned at Carcassonne. Some time after, he left for Italy with his regiment.

[…][216] and the formidable stature of men in this elite troop. Napoleon's astonishment only ceased when he was named the master of arms.

The first bout between Lafaugère and Count Bondy took place in 1814 before a large audience.

It was an event which fascinated the fencing world as at the time Count Bondy was considered as the period's strongest amateur.

He was left-handed and of a very tall stature.

Count Bondy presented himself to fence in fanciful costume.[217]

He had dressed in a suit of stitched white satin and wore around his neck a lace collar, the ends of which fell like cravats on his breast.

The bout was done in two stages: Lafaugère touched Count Bondy forty-eight times and was only touched three times.

This famous bout inspired in Frédéric Régamey the subject of a watercolour which was the sensation of the Painting Salon of 1886.

The painter of the Academy of Arms brought to the fore[218] Lafaugère touching Count Bondy with a strike vigorously carried. In the background,[219] the spectators, to the number of ninety, representing images of fencing[220] in the 19th century, masters and amateurs, all made after authentic portraits.

Under the Restoration, fencing enjoyed in France the greatest favour.

---

[214] *dignes de foi*
[215] *chasseurs à cheval*
[216] Some text is missing from the original
[217] *une tenue des plus fantaisistes*
[218] *a mis au premier plan*
[219] *au second plan*
[220] *les illustrations de l'escrime*

At Paris notably, outside the fencing halls, certain owners of concert halls, of cafes, made their rooms available to amateurs.

There, the first come fencer made a tour of the assembly presenting a foil. This was the form used for engaging the fencers to measure themselves with him.

Lafaugère appeared one day in one of these meetings, accompanied by some friends. One presented the foil to one of those who declined the offer and indicated Lafaugère as champion but without naming him.

Lafaugère accepted and said while buttoning his jacket, "You will not have any pleasure bouting with me as my master warned me that I would never touch anyone but that, however, I would never be touched."

His adversary laughed much at this prediction and promised himself to make [this statement a] lie.

The two fencers put themselves in guard and the bout ended without a single strike touched on one side or the other.

A second fencer presented himself, believing to be more lucky:[221] same result.

The astonishment of the audience was at its height, none knowing Lafaugère.

During these two bouts, a military master of arms struggling to attract his attention, said very loudly, "Me, on such a strike, I would have done this. On such another, I would have done that."

In brief, this master full of confidence in himself went to bout with Lafaugère, who had regained his place, and prayed him, if he did not feel too fatigued, of doing him the honour of fencing with him.

Lafaugère, who had agreed to the proposal of this master, accepted courteously the invitation. But this time, his adversary received a hail of strikes with the point.[222]

Distraught, he tried to recognise in the middle of the avalanche the strikes, head shots,[223] parries and lightning ripostes. It was in vain. The bout ends without him able to touch Lafaugère's chest.

Shamed by his lack of success,[224] the poor master of arms said to Lafaugère, "your master has well assured that you will never be touched, and yet ..." "I understand nothing here," responded Lafaugère smiling. "It is the first time that this happened to me."

---

[221] *plus heureux*
[222] *de bouton*
[223] *couronnements*
[224] *insuccès*

The name Lafaugère, pronounced then by one of his friends, gave the solution to the puzzle. This name, so well-known by fencing amateurs, was saluted by enthusiastic acclamation on the part of the spectators that the three consecutive bouts had been very intriguing.

At the time of his duel with Bertrand, Lafaugère went to the meeting, hands behind his back, veritably dawdling.

A confederate, who went there interested, met him. Surprised to see Lafaugère alone, he asked him where were his witnesses. "I will find enough of them down there," responded Lafaugère. Actually, a great number of masters of arms had gathered on the place of combat and Lafaugère soon found two witnesses.

In this duel, Bertrand received a wound, happily not serious[225].

Lafaugère was the premier force in pistols and his ball hit with each shot a five franc piece that someone had thrown in the air.

We have said that Lafaugère was a painter. When one of his works struck in a manner the particular attention of a visitor and attracted to him (Lafaugère) some compliment: "If this painting pleases you," he said, "you please me by accepting it."

And if, with discretion, the person refuses, "Speak of it no more," replied then Lafaugère, "I am sorry to be a bore."[226]

In his *Traité de l'Art de Faire des Armes* [Treatise on the Art of Using Arms], Lafaugère, making allusion to La Boëssière's treatise, published two years before his, said,

> I believe that the old methods are irrevocably worn out,[227] but it seems that one would bring them back to us.
>
> A system that the ancients had adopted of frequently using the left hand reappears again in a new treatise. I am very far from approving this method, as it is vicious and even dangerous to all persons who engage themselves in the Art of arms.
>
> This method causes confusion by removing the limits that one has fixed in the principles; that which leads even in an affair of honour, to a baseness made by a false bravado which does not fit the French character, etc.

One sees by that which preceded that Lafaugère is the first who forbade the use of the left hand.

---

[225] *sans gravité*
[226] *importun*
[227] *étaient usées sans retour*

We have extracted from the *L'Esprit de l'escrime, poème didactique* [The Spirit of Fencing: a didactic poem] the several lines which follow in order to give an overview of the famous master's second work.

> From French Parnassus, the daring author:
> I will not climb the frightening heights;
> I only borrow the help of rhyme,
> To make attractive the rules of fencing
> To depict the spirit and the deep calculations.
> [...]
> But do not think that the aim of fencing
> May be construed to aid those planning[228] a crime.
> No, it's task, more beautiful, is to capitalise[229]
> The faculties of the body and those of the mind.
> [...]
>
> **Sword-Rattling**[230]
>
> [...]
> These rivals distance all desire to parry,
> In order to attack looking to make a shove,
> They throw themselves furiously, blindly, menacingly,
> And from the iron spring sparkling fires.
> Not content with these shocks produced against nature,
> They bend the iron even down to the mounting
> And the iron curves itself under the force of their arms
> Into a frightening hoop, hisses and flies in sparks!
> In the instant the section, the foolhardy hand
> Anew comes to beat the body of the adversary
> At this barely legal strike, thrown so abruptly,
> The opponent indignant, in his inattention,
> Confronts the danger, with head bowed,
> Throws himself, furious, losing all thought,
> Pushes without reflection,[231] his bent arm[232]
> Maintaining the combat, the end of mercy.
> But if the strike is not too severe

---

[228] *médite*
[229] *de mettre à profit*
[230] *Le Ferraillement*
[231] *a tort, a travers*
[232] *son bras raccourci*

And that it may be sent by a light hand
The strike is not received, you will understand therefore
That it should, well thrown, pass through the body.

---

Lafaugère preserved for Jean Daressy, his master and friend, the liveliest gratitude. He dedicated to his memory "The Spirit of Fencing"[233] the following quatrain:

Generous Daressy, in the eternal night,
Time does not take the talents, the blessings.
In the sighs of my heart your memory is mixed
Like your glory in my success.

# Jean-Louis

Under the title of Master of Arms under the Restoration, Vigeant, one of the most prominent figures occluded by Jean-Louis, traced in emotive terms the life of the celebrated master of Montpellier. We cannot do better than to send the reader to this book.

We say only that Jean-Louis, one of the most illustrious school heads of this century, was born at Saint-Domingue in 1785 and that he was a mulatto like the Knight Saint-George.

In 1793, Jean-Louis was brought to France. Three years later, he was admitted to a regiment as a child of the company.[234] The Master of Arms, named d'Érape, having recognised the good disposition of the little mulatto, took him under his protection and taught him at his school.

In 1814, we find Jean-Louis the first master of the 32nd Line Regiment, garrisoned at Madrid. It is thus that he was the hero of an epic duel recounted by Vigeant, the duel in which Jean-Louis fought thirteen consecutive times, without intermission, and put his thirteen adversaries out of the fight.

He entered, in 1816, the 3rd Engineers Regiment, with which he went consecutively from Metz to Arras and from Arras to Montpellier.

It is in this last town that Jean-Louis took his retirement and opened a fencing hall celebrated among those of the Midi of France. That was in 1830.

---

[233] *l'Éspirit de l'Escrime*
[234] *enfant de troupe*

Jean-Louis gave lessons until 1885, a period in which he became blind and sadly lost his wife. He carried with resignation his first misfortune [but] he could not survive the loss of her company. On 19 Novembre of the same year, Jean-Louis was no more.

# Bertrand

François-Joseph Bertrand, one of the great figures of fencing in the 19th century, was born at Paris in 1796.

He was the son and student of the master who published in 1801 a small-scale[235] treatise having the title "Fencing Applied to the Military Art".

Bertrand, first associated with his father, opened alone in 1823 a fencing hall in the rue Saint-Thomas-du-Louvre. It was in this period that he was named instructor[236] in one of the Bodyguard Companies (Company Gramont).

On 7 October 1827, the fencing teachers attempted to revive the ancient Community suppressed by the Revolution. Bertrand was named president and Blot secretary of this new Community which carried the title "The Society of Arms of Paris," and only lived a very short time.

Bertrand had a prodigious speed of hand. He had the habit, in order to exercise himself, of making double counters with a foil having two blades welded one to the other.

After completing a long glorious career, Bertrand died at Paris on 18 August 1876.

Pierre Prévost and Robert the Elder, whom both were fencing teachers in Paris, must be counted in the number of Bertrand's best students.

> Monsieur,
>
> Knowing that the appreciation of any art is not strange to you and M Achille Ricour having told me that it would be agreeable to you to attend an assault of arms,[237] I pray you accept the two tickets enclosed which I have addressed to you.
>
> I dare to hope, Monsieur, that you would honour us with your presence.

---

[235] *de peu d'étendue*
[236] *professeur civil*
[237] *un assaut d'armes*

Accept, Monsieur, the high consideration of your humble servant,

Bertrand

Fencing Teacher of the Royal School
Paris, this 22 February 1840

These tickets were for the assault given the day after by Mille, Daressy and Lozès the younger in the hall of the Wauxhall d'Été (located on the boulevard Saint-Martin.)

Here is the program of the bouts:

**First Part**
Mille and Raimondi
Marcellin and Lozès the younger
Pons and Mille
Prévost and Daressy

**Second Part**
Alliac and Lozès the younger
Daressy and Bonnet
Pons and Prévost
Bertrand and Lozès

# Assault of Arms in 1814

Sir Mathieu Coulon, Master of Deeds of Arms, advises the public that he has the honour of giving an Assault on Sunday 2 September 1814 in which we will see several distinguished masters and amateurs, from both the Capital and the Provinces.

For a long time, Paris has been deprived of this type of entertainment, which must be all the more enjoyable to the amateurs as it offers them the occasion of testing their talents in the Art so essentially associated with the education of French youth.

This bout will take place at *Wauxhall d'Été* boulevard Bondi,[238] behind the Château-d'Eau from one until four in the afternoon.

Price of entry is from 3 francs per person.

The assault will be opened by Messers. Compoint and Prévost, the first, Master of Deeds of Arms of the Capital, and the second, of the town of Rouen.

---

[238] Original footnote: Boulevard Saint-Martin

Pierre Darressy

Second Bout: Messers. Mathieu Coulon and Philippe.

Third Bout: Messer. Brémond and Antonin Gomard.

Fourth Bout: M. Bouiliet, Master of Deeds of Arms, will fence with M. Bertrand junior.

Fifth Bout: M. Mathieu Coulon will make a second assault with M. Brémond.

Several amateurs will do me the honour of fencing with me.

The bouts will be ended by Messers. Mathieu Coulons and Antonin Gomard.

# Pierre Daressy

Pierre Daressy was born in Agen on 26 July 1806. His father, Jean Daressy, taught him to fence[239] at an early age and, as he had already attained a remarkable strength, he constrained him for two years to only fence the counters, without making a single attack.

In 1822, Pierre Daressy entered as apprentice dyer in the house of an old family friend named Serres, where he remained around fifteen months. Then he quit Agen in order to make, according to the habit, his tour of France, in order than he perfect himself in his trade and learn all the secrets of it.

He visited consecutively Toulouse, Carcassonne, Béziers, Montpellier, Nîmes, Avignon, Valence and Lyon.

In his wanderings, Daressy occupied himself little with cochineal and indigo, the foil was more attractive for him, and in all the towns in which he stayed he did bout after bout with fencing masters and amateurs.

Success encouraging him, Daressy abandoned dying completely, came to Carcassonne and opened a fencing hall there.

But eighteen months after, experiencing the desire to see again his family, he gave up his fencing hall to one of his students named Journet and returned to Agen. His absence had lasted five years.

A short time later, Daressy came to Paris and descended upon Lafaugère who maintained a fencing hall at 19 rue de l'École-de-Médecine.

Having learned that the master of arms of a Royal Guard Regiment was on the point of retiring, Daressy solicited the post[240] which would become vacant. The colonel, after having seen him fence and give a lesson, immediately accorded it to him and, on 29 May 1829, Daressy signed the contract which named him for eight years the first master of fencing of the Light Cavalry[241] of the Guard.

He was then in his twenty-third year.

It is in this period that he made his first bout with Bertrand, president of the Society of the Fencing Teachers of Paris, and, more committed, in the role of civil master of arms to the Body Guard (Company Gramont) in which a cousin of Daressy named Rouilles had a part.

Between two lessons, this cousin spoke to Bertrand of the fencing

---

[239] *à faire des armes*
[240] *l'emploi*
[241] *chasseurs à cheval*

talent of the Cavalry's young master and asked if he would be agreeable to bouting with him.

Bertrand having responded drily: "I will not fence with soldiers." Rouillès put to him that his cousin was a master of arms and by consequence a colleague.

The Bodyguards present at this meeting joined their comrade and pointed out[242] to Bertrand that they too were soldiers and that his response was no less unkind to them than to Daressy.

In order to repair this blunder which he had committed, Bertrand had to accept the bout which took place some days later.

The two fencers undertook a bout full of pride. Success was, moreover, shared.

After the bout, Bertrand could not help saying to his opponent with a touch of bad temper, "You are not stronger than the others." "It is possible, monsieur," responded Daressy. "But I just proved that I am as strong as you."

The incident had no further consequences and the question of this unhappy bout was never raised between the two masters who became excellent friends and who, more than once, measured themselves in public.

In 1830, after the disbanding of the Royal Guard, Daressy returned to Agen. But, solicited by several of his students, former officers of Light Cavalry, who had retaken service in the 4th Regiment of Lancers recently formed, he did not delay in entering this corps with the title of first master and the rank of sergeant.

Daressy left military service in 1834 and opened a fencing hall in Paris, 20 rue Jean-Jacques-Rousseau. The reputation which he already enjoyed soon attracted to him numerous students.

From 1834 to 1855, Pierre Daressy remained constantly on the go,[243] teaching his art with dedication and preaching by example in numerous public bouts which took place[244] at Wauxhall and at Salle Montesquieu.

He took part in this constellation of brilliant fencers who were named Bertrand, Bonnet, Lozès the Elder, Pons, Prévost, Raimondi, etc. These masters made for themselves a duty of transmitting to their successors the good traditions that they had received from their forebears,[245] bringing to the art of fencing certain improvements, the fruit of their long experience.

---

[242] *faire observer*
[243] *constamment sur la brèche* – constantly in the breach?
[244] *se donnèrent*
[245] *devanciers*

In 1855, Daressy contracted cataracts and completely lost his sight.

Despite his blindness, he occasionally gave lessons. He possessed a *sentiment du fer* to such a degree that he knew how to tell, by the engagement, whether the student's position was correct.

Some years later, another master of arms, Jean-Louis, having lost his sight also, repeated this prodigy.

In 1860, Daressy gave up his salle and said goodbye to the art which he had loved and cultivated for forty-two years.

Daressy was of a lofty stature (1.78m). He had a well proportioned body, an unusual muscular strength and very great suppleness.

The physical means which nature had given him served him marvellously in the career that he had chosen.

Very fond of music, he occupied his leisure in playing the violin with a remarkable talent.

Pierre Daressy was in his sixty-fifth year when he died at Paris on 3 July 1871. His funeral was in the Saint-Eugène church in the middle of many assistants, among which were found Bertrand, Pons, Robert the Elder, Mimiague, Hamel, Ardohain and several other masters of arms, hastening in order to pay their last respects to he who showed himself in all circumstances the best of comrades.

At Pierre Daressy's school were trained[246] a certain number of good teachers. Among them we cite Berrier, who was associated with Robert the Elder; then Hamel, the first fencing teacher of the circle of the artistic union; Leroy, first master of the 8th Dragoons who was decorated for his conduct on battlefield of the Crimea and died captain.

Pierre Daressy's principal students were: Messers the Duke of Rohan, prince of Léon, marquis of Choiseul, baron Goualès, captain Devaux, baron Beaumont, de Lauvergnac, de Brouart, Capelle, Obin (of the Opera), marquis of Richepanse, de Fiers, de Guimaraës, Méchain, General the Count of Clerambault, Dupin de Clappîer, baron Vigier, Auguste and Frédéric Huber, Count of Ribes, count and viscount of Ruty, Ney of Moscow, Ségur d'Aguesseau, Eugène Cart, viscount Ségur, de Montherol, count of Angle-Beaumanoir, de Firmas, viscount Châteaurenard, Edouard Broustet, the musician Tolbecque, count Martin (du Nord) junior, baron Léon Michel de Trétaigne, Estur, de Brémond, colonel José Rosas, marquis de Menilglaize, baron Roullin, de Saint-Clair, nephew of prince Orlof, Paul and Alphonse Varin, Palant, de la Nauze, Etienne and Fernand Giraudeau, de Chaniérac, de Neugarède, de Ramond, de Prados,

---

[246] *se formèrent*

prince Ghika, de Tescourt, de la Comble, de Montozon, colonel Rey, prince of Craon, de Ginestous, Cousin de Feugré, the commander of Saint-Victor, prince of Berghes, de la Rochefoucauld, de Chabannes, de Froissard, de Fitz-James, de Bressieux, etc.

Pierre Daressy was, finally, a fencing teacher for several houses of education.

Among the provosts who assisted Daressy, we must mention Ardohain, the dean of masters of arms of the 19th century, who died in 1885 at the age of 81 years.

## Academy of Arms (1886)

The fencing teachers of Paris formed at the end of the year 1886, under the title of Academy of Arms, a society composed of

**Honorary Master**
Tenured
Deputy

**Honorary Members**
Corresponding
Military

Each recipient receives a warrant[247] signed by the committee.

Hippolyte Gatechair was the first president of this Academy which numbers today 140 members.

The committee is composed currently of Messers the Minister of War, honorary president; Jacob, president; Berges, vice-president; Vigeant, treasurer; Georges Robert, secretary; Rouleau, Collin, Prévost and Haller.

---

[247] Original footnote: The original watercolour of this warrant is due to the brush of Frédéric Régamey

# Duels and Letters of Remission

## Duel between François de Vivonne, Lord of Chateigneraie and Guy Chabot, Baron of Jarnac

1547

Towards the end of the reign of François I, the rumour spread at Court that Guy Chabot, baron of Jarnac and Montlieu, boasted of having "good relations"[248] with his mother-in-law, Madeleine de Puy-Guyon, second wife of Charles Chabot.

In a moment of largesse, Jarnac confided to the Dauphin that he obtained all that he desired from his mother-in-law, wanting to say that she had given him the money that he needed.

The Dauphin divulged the secret to a woman who communicated it to other persons so that from mouth-to-mouth all the Court soon knew it.

Only the story was enlarged and became injurious to the honour of Madeleine de Puy-Guyon.

Jarnac wanted to trace the source of these hurtful words.

The Dauphin was going to be compromised. François de Vivonne, lord of Chateigneraie, came to his rescue.

In the hope of gaining the favour of the prince, in recompense of the service that he was going to render, La Chateigneraie announced to whomever wanted to hear that it was to himself that Jarnac had made this confidence.

---

[248] A euphemism, obviously

The latter seized the first occasion which presented itself in order to say in a meeting that he who had invented this slander had lied, making well understood that his words were addressed to La Chateigneraie.

The word was immediately reported to La Chateigneraie who demanded from François I permission to fight Jarnac in the lists.

The king refused giving several reasons, among them: "that a prince should not allow a thing to be an issue from which one cannot hope for good."

But hardly had François I died than his successor, solicited by the two enemy lords, gave the permission refused by the king his father.

La Chateigneraie, then aged twenty-six years, was renown for his strength. He had devoted himself early to all bodily exercise, particularly to fencing. His father, the grand seneschal of Poitou, had given him a master of arms directly from Italy [at] "whatever it may cost", says Brantôme in his *Mémoires*.

Jarnac, less robust than his adversary, had nonetheless acquired a great reputation for bravery for his fine conduct at the battle of Cérisoles (1544).[249]

These two lords, distantly related,[250] raised together at the court of King Francis I, had always lived as good companions in arms.

Their duel took place on 10 July 1547 in the presence of the king and the court. The field was dressed near the park of Saint-Germain-en-Laye.

La Chateigneraie's second was the Count of Aumale (François de Guise) and that of Jarnac was Claude Gouffier, baron of Boisy, grand squire.

The usual ceremonies, consisting mainly in the reception and showing of the weapons and armour, began at six in the morning and lasted well into the day. Then the two adversaries swore the accustomed oath on the holy gospels and, after each of them received a sword and two daggers, the Constable (Anne de Montmorency) gave the attack signal by crying out three times "Let them go, the good fighters!"[251]

La Chateigneraie and Jarnac threw themselves at each other covering themselves with their swords from the great thrusts and cutting strikes.

---

[249] A battle in the Italian Wars (1542-46) outside the village of Ceresole d'Alba in the Piedmont region of Italy between France and the combined Spain and Holy Roman Empire

[250] *un peu parents*

[251] *Laissez les aller, les bons combattants!*

La Chateigneraie received the first cutting strike on the hamstring of the left leg[252] then a second in the same place, which put him in a state unable to continue the fight.

Jarnac, in this instant, was master of his adversary's life. But he showed a great moderation and praised the wounded to the king saying, "Sire, halt it. I give it you for the love of God and yourself."

Henri II, surprised along with all the court at the unexpected result of the duel, was hesitant. It was only at the insistence of the winner and on the prayers of the great officers that he threw his baton onto the arena, putting an end to the combat.

Henri II addressed himself to Jarnac: "You have done your duty," he said, "and are given your honour."

The Constable, Grand Admiral and Marshals of France asked the king that the winner be brought to his house in triumph. But Claude Gouffier, Jarnac's second, refused and said to Henri that it was sufficient that the winner was in the good graces of His Majesty. Jarnac, taking the floor to speak, assured the king that he desired nothing more than to be his servant.

Henri II, touched by Jarnac's conduct, brought him close, embraced him and said to him, "You fought like Caesar and spoke like Cicero."

La Chateigneraie could not bear this humiliation. In a fit of rage, he tore at the bandages on his injuries and died three days later.

## The Coup de Jarnac

The duel in which Guy Chabot vanquished La Chateigneraie gave birth to a new saying: "to make or bear the Coup de Jarnac," implying the idea of betrayal. It is, in effect, a prejudice still generally widespread that Jarnac could only have owed his victory to an unfair strike, known to him alone, that which one vulgarly calls a "secret strike."[253]

We serve the cause of truth in combating this error that persons who are otherwise on top of all things fencing do not share and they know that the slicing strike and the reverse to the hamstring is found taught in the treatises of the sixteenth century.

We give below the account of a duel, pre-dating that of Jarnac where one of the combatants died of injuries that he received to the hamstring.

---

[252] *le jarret de la jambe gauche*
[253] *une botte secrète*

The facts that we have reported and the words spoken by the king after the defeat of La Chateigneraie sufficiently prove that Guy Chabot of Jarnac fought according to the laws of honour and that he comported himself as a gentleman in not abusing his victory and in refusing the triumph to which he had the right.

Another proof in support is that a fortnight after the duel when Henri II was consecrated at Reims, it was Jarnac who during all the ceremony had the honour of carrying the golden spur of the Knight-King.

A little time after, Guy Chabot, baron of Jarnac, lord of Saint-Gelais, Montlieu and Saint-Aulaye, knight of the order of the king,[254] became first gentleman of the chambre, governor of the provinces of Aunis and Saintoge, perpetual mayor of Bordeaux, captain of the Château of Hâ and sénéchal of Périgord.

We possess an account signed in his hand in August 1549 from the king for the awarding of 1,000 *livres tournois* per year as captain of forty lances of Ordonnance.

A granddaughter of Jarnac, Eléonore Chabot, married Louis de Vivonne, lord of La Chateigneraie.

Thus ended the quarrel between the two families.

---

[254] Almost certainly the *Ordre de Saint-Michel* created in 1469 by Louis XI rather than the *Ordre du Saint-Esprit* create by Henry III in 1578, both known as the orders of the king.

## The Duel of a Seventeen-Year-Old Page (1540)

In the course of January 1540, King François I received at Chantilly Emperor Charles V. During this stay, a squire of the king's daughters named René de Sajault, aged around seventeen years, and a king's guard having met in the courtyard of the château and began joking. The joking became insults and soon a quarrel so acrimonious to the point that they challenged each other. They went to fight in the corner of a park a little distance from the château.

> "They unsheathed their swords together from which they hurled several strikes one on the other so that the said supplicant (René de Sajault) was injured by the said deceased in two places in the face and the said deceased with a cutting strike to the hamstring in which he had some nerves cut."

The guard died about a month after "without lacking for good treatment, good regimen, government or otherwise."

King François I absolved René de Sajault in favour of his youth and accorded him a Letter of Remission given at Paris in the month of July 1540.

## The Duel of Des Bordes against d'Ivoy-Genlis (1560)

In 1560, a nephew of the Marshall of Bourdillon, named Des Bordes, battled in a duel near the park of Saint-Germain-en-Laye with d'Ivoy-Genlis. Des Bordes had a hamstring cut but he didn't die of it. He was killed two years later in the battle of Dreux.

## Letter of Challenge from Lord Castel-Bayart

(XVI century)

Monsieur, you are such a little thing that were it not for the insolence of your words I would never have remembered you.

The bearer will tell you where I am with two swords of which you may have the choice.

If you have the confidence to come here, I will take the trouble to return you.

(*Mémoires de Brantôme*)

## Letter Addressed to the Tribunal of the Marshals of France

I have the honour to declare to our lords the Marshals of France who yesterday found me with M de Crosby and in our interview believing to perceive a lack of process towards someone who interests me, I thought that it was my duty to bear witness to my sensibility in the arrangements as honour dictates.

Paris, 19 June 1785
The Master Caccia-Fiatti

## Admonition Obtained by the Baron of Gourgue

(25 November 1671)

(*The first part of the original piece is written in Latin*)

Henry by Divine Mercy and the grace of the Holy Apostolic See, Archbishop of Bordeaux, Primate of Aquitaine to you and to all priests submitting to our jurisdiction, greetings in the Lord. In the incident of the very noble Sir Armand de Gourgue, king's counsellor in his councils and lieutenant general of the senechalship of Guyenne, we command you to publish that if anyone has knowledge of the things contained in the Letters here below written in French, they have to say or make known that which they know and this within the space of six days from the publication of this present admonition. Otherwise, [they will] be denounced and may be excommunicated.

Given at Bordeaux in our council on the 25th of the month of November of the year of our Lord 1671.

By the authority of Monsignor Archbishop of Bordeaux and Primate of Aquitaine.

At the insistence and request of Sir Armand de Gourgue, king's councillor in his councils, lieutenant general of the senechalship of Guyenne, it is commanded to the first priest on this request to admonish on pain of excommunication whoever knows that on the thirtieth of the month of October last the said Sir, the complainant, was at the port of Cambes in order to load the wine of monsieur the president of Gourgue, his father, and it occurred that a certain person hindered the workers loading the said wine. The said supplicant remonstrated with him that he [the complainant] ought not be used in this manner. Nonetheless, the said person wanted to lead the workers to his house by the force of strikes of the baton and sword with threat of wounding[255] them most grievously.

Item: that knowing the said person had called the said complainant insolent and that there was no comparison to be made with him and that he wanted to be served first.

Item: that the said person blaspheming the holy name of God boasting that he wanted to mistreat him wherever he would find him and for this effect asked for his pistols and horse saying to the said supplicant that if he were an honest man he would find himself alone on the next road where he would wait to fight with him.

Item: knowing the said person or other thing mentioned above, he will reveal it within six days after the publication or notification of this instrument otherwise he will be denounced [and] excommunicated.

Henry, Archbishop of Bordeaux

In the margin, the archbishop added in his hand "a civil end."

# Letter of Pardon Accorded to Etienne de Clugny of Praslay, Councillor in the Court of the Parliament of Dijon

(as witness)

(30 Mars 1718)

Louis[256] by the grace of God King of France and Navarre, to all those who will see these present letters, greetings.

We have received the humble supplication of our beloved and loyal Etienne of Clugny de Praslay, Councillor of our court of the parliament of Dijon, making profession of the Catholic religion, apostolic

---
[255] *excéder*
[256] Louis XV

and Roman, outlining that on the night of the 29th to 30th July last, he found himself with Sir Philibert Jehannin de Chamblan, also a councillor in the said Parliament, and Claude Varenne, lawyer, in the Place Royale in the said town, the usual location for a promenade where Sir Pourcher, master of accounts, was with a woman his wife and other persons with whom the said Sir Pourcher had dined. After having made several turns of the said Place, the supplicant was surprised that the said Sir Pourcher pulled him aside from the company where he was and conducted him some steps away, telling him that he had insulted him and that he wished to see him sword in hand. The supplicant, who did not expect such a speech since he had neither incited any provocation nor otherwise, contented himself to say to Sir Pourcher that he did not use a sword but only the stick or cane that he carried and that it was wrong that he had attacked him. Sir Pourcher, angered by this response, went to complain to the company that he had just left, saying that the supplicant and the said Varenne had treated him like a commoner. He gave the place to the lady wife of the said Sir Pourcher and to those of his company, asking the supplicant and the said Sir Jehannin and Varenne with whom he was that which had passed between them and the said Sir Pourcher, at which the said Sir Jehannin spoke assuring Mrs Pourcher that he had not thought to offend the said Sir Pourcher. This was repeated and confirmed by the said supplicant and that the said Sir Pourcher should be content with that which had been said to the lady his wife which had taken place to the satisfaction of all others who may believe themselves offended. He left the woman despite all efforts that she made to hold him. According to him, he went to his house to take a defensive sword[257] that he hid under his doublet. He came to look for the said supplicant and the said Varenne in the said Place Royale, where neither being found there nor in the other neighbouring streets that he roamed because, no longer thinking of him, they had left the said Place in order to retire each to his home. They met in the rue St-Etienne near the house of Varenne's father. He came looking for them just in front of Varenne's house where they talked together quietly. And having perceived them, he affected to pass near them and push rudely the said supplicant looking for an occasion to maltreat him and the said Varenne, with the result that the said Sir Pourcher drew the sword that he had hidden in his arm, obliging the said Varenne to draw the little duelling sword that he was accustomed to carry and put himself in defence against the strikes that Sir Pourcher made at him and by

---

[257] une épée de defense

which the said Varenne was injured in several places. In this situation, the supplicant believed himself obliged to separate them by running to them with no other weapon than his cane and not leaving them during all the time that the action lasted, wherein the said Sir Pourcher injured the said Varenne with three or four strikes. He found himself injured by two strikes. The supplicant, neither knowing how these strikes had been given in all these tumultuous movements, nor saying "Hold, Varenne, see Pourcher is struck"[258] nor other terms or words in the frightful trouble where he was in the heat of the action, and in the violent agitations which accompanied it, where his own life was not safe, having no weapon and finding himself equally exposed to the strikes of the two combatants. Nonetheless, the said Sir Pourcher, being deceased from his wounds some time after, was examined by Parliament and the Lieutenant-Criminal of Dijon who ruled against the supplicant and the said Varenne.

But in the view of the inheritors of the said Sir Pourcher, recognising that he brought this misfortune on himself [by going] to his house to take his sword in order to maltreat the said Varenne and the supplicant without any cause and in the time that the noise had ceased, they treated the civil interests with regard to the supplicant [and] that of the said Varenne, and they desist from all pursuit by act here attached under our counter seal. By our Letters of the month of March of the present year, we have accorded to the said Varenne grace, remission and pardon, that which the supplicant obliged as being present at the action, also having recourse to our clemency made very humble supplication to us, wanting to accord himself our Letters of Pardon on these necessities.

For these reasons, desiring to prefer mercy to the rigour of justice, on the advice of our very dear and very loved uncle the Duke of Orléans, grandson of the Regent, and by our special grace, full royal power and authority, we have acquitted and pardoned the said supplicant and by these present signs in our hand we quit and pardon the deed and case here above, with all fines and corporal offences, civil and criminal, that he may have incurred with regard to us and justice. We make void all decrees, defaults, contumaces, awards, judgements and injunctions which may have occurred by reason of this. We put him back into his good and healthy reputation, and into his goods not otherwise confiscated, satisfaction made to the civil party if they had been or if it is necessary. We impose this restitution on our Procurer General, his substitutes, present and to come, and to all others. So, we

---

[258] *tiens Varenne, voilà, Pourcher, touché*

command to our beloved and faithful councillors, the people holding our Parliament at Dijon, the result of the deed and case here above occurring, that these present, having been ratified, and the supplicant being content to enjoy and use them plainly, peacefully and perpetually, ceasing and making to cease all troubles and contrary hindrances, to charge him with representing himself before you in three months, under pain of being deprived of the effects hereunto. Because such is our pleasure. In witness of which, we have put our seal to these present [letters].

Given at Paris, the thirtieth day of March, Year of Grace one thousand seven hundred eighteen and in our third reign.

Louis

For the King:

The Duke of Orléans, current regent

Phelypeaux

In the margin is found the following mention: "Donation,[259] five hundred livres."

---

[259] *aumône*

LongEdge Press publishes quality translations of French texts of interest to the scholar and practitioner of historical fencing. Visit LongEdge Press at www.longedgepress.com for more books, articles on items of historical interest and practical guides.

**Secrets of the Sword Alone** Henri de Sainct-Didier (1573)

**Fencing Through the Ages** Adolphe Corthey (1898), including his report on the *Transformation de l'Épée de Combat* (1894) and several contemporary newspaper reports of his public demonstrations of historical fencing.

***La Canne Royale*** Larribeau, Humé, comprising Larribeau's *Nouvelle Théorie du Jeu de la Canne* (1856) and Humé's *Traité et Théorie de Canne Royale* (1862)

**The Art of Fencing** Jean de Brye (1721)

**Fencing Manual** Ministry of War (1877)

**Manual of Contre-Pointe Fencing** Joseph Tinguely (1856) with a foreword by Julian Garry of *De Taille et d'Estoc*

www.ingramcontent.com/pod-product-compliance
Lightning Source LLC
Chambersburg PA
CBHW031959080426
42735CB00007B/449